Cla≤

G. T. HAWKER

Spell it yourself

Oxford University Press

Oxford University Press, Great Clarendon Street, Oxford, OX2 6DP

Oxford New York
Athens Auckland Bangkok Bogotá Buenos Aires
Calcutta Cape Town Chennai Dar es Salaam
Delhi Florence Hong Kong Istanbul Karachi
Kuala Lumpur Madrid Melbourne Mexico City
Mumbai Nairobi Paris São Paulo Singapore
Taipei Tokyo Toronto

and associated companies in
Berlin Ibadan

Oxford is a trade mark of Oxford University Press

© G. T. Hawker 1981

First published in paperback 1962
Second edition in paperback 1981
Redesigned impression for paperback 1994

First published in hardback 1992
Redesigned impression for hardback 1995

paperback   10 9 8
hardback   10 9 8 7 6

ISBN 0 19 910342 9 (paperback)
ISBN 0 19 834138 5 (hardback)

A CIP catalogue record for this book is available from the British Library

Printed in Great Britain by The Bath Press, Bath

Contents

Instructions

1   Think hard about the word you wish to spell and try to decide with which two letters it starts.

2   Find these two letters in the Index and you will see the number of the page where the word can be found or where you should begin looking for it.

3   Turn to this page and look down the column under these two letters until you find the word you want. Where there are a lot of words which begin with the same two letters, the first three letters of the words are given at the top of the column to help you find the word you want.

It may be necessary to add the word endings shown in *italics* on the right-hand side of the column in order to build up the complete word you want, e.g.

rich   *er, est, ly, ness, es*
hair   *dresser, -dryer, pin, -slide, -style, s*

Here the words **richer, richest, richly, richness** and **riches** may be built up, and also **hairdresser(s), hair-dryer(s), hairpins(s), hair-slide(s), hair-style(s)** and **hairs.**

Where the last letter or letters of a word are in *italics* these must be left off before adding to the other endings, e.g.

happ*y*   *ier, iest, ily, iness.*

Here the *y* must be left off before making:

happier, happiest, happily, happiness.

The plurals of most nouns may be formed by adding the letter, or letters, shown in *italics* on the extreme right of the column. A few nouns have their plurals given in full on the right of the column, and you will notice that some nouns have two plurals, either of which may be used, e.g. **cactuses** or **cacti, hoofs** or **hooves, fish** or **fishes.**

All the words with *ed, ing* after them are verbs or may be used as verbs. If you require the word to end in either *ed* or *ing*, remember the following:

(a) **kick** *ed*, *ing*, *s* = **kicked kicking kicks**

Here *ed* or *ing* or *s* may be added to the verb without changing the word at all.

(b) **stab** *bed*, *bing*, *s* = **stabbed stabbing stabs**
    st̶op *ped*, *ping*, *s* = **stopped stopping stops**

Here you can see that the final consonant (the last letter) of these verbs has to be doubled before adding *ed* or *ing*.

(c) **blame** *d*, *ȩing*, *s* = **blamed blaming blames**

Where a verb ends in a letter **e** the *d* or *s* may be added to the word but the **e** must be dropped before adding *ing*. An *ȩ* is placed before the *ing* to remind you of this.

There are a few other verbs which change their endings in different ways. You will usually find these endings printed by the side of, above or below, the verb, e.g.

began		**lie**	*d, s*	**carry**	*ing*
begin	*ning, s*	**lying**		**carr** *ied*	*ies*
begun					

Warning: A word which has a star (*) after it has the same sound, or almost the same sound, as another word; but it has a different meaning and spelling, e.g. **knew* new*; their* there*; which* witch*.** The word endings will help you to decide which of these words you want and so will the words in brackets. These are included to guide you; they are not always exact definitions. The words are paired in small print at the bottom of the page. If you find that you have looked up the wrong word you may easily see how the other is spelt and where it may be found in its correct alphabetical place in the book.

ab

abandon	*ed, ing, ment, s*
abate	*d, ∮ing, ment, s*
abbess	*es*
abbey	*s*
abbot	*s*
abduct	*ed, ing, ion, s*
abhor	*red, ring, rence, rent, s*
abide	*d, ∮ing, s*
ability	*ies*
ablaze	
able	*r, st, -bodied*
abnormal	*ity, ly*
aboard	
abolish	*ed, ing, es*
abominable	
abominate	*d, ∮ing, s*
Aboriginal	*s or* **Aborigines**
abound	*ed, ing, s*
about	
above	*-board*
abreast	
abroad	
abrupt	*ly, ness*
abscess	*es*
absence	*s*
absent	*ed, ing, ly, ee, s*
absent-minded	*ly, ness*
absolute	*ly*
absorb	*ed, ing, ent, s*
abstain	*ed, ing, s*
absurd	*ity, ly*
abundance	
abundant	*ly*
abuse	*d, ∮ing, s*
abysmal	*ly*
abyss	*es*

ac

academy	*ies*
accelerate	*d, ∮ing, s*
accent	*s*
accept* (receive)	*able, ed, ing, s*
accident	*al, ally, s*
accommodate	*d, ∮ing, s*
accommodation	
accompany	*ing*
accompan *ied*	*ies*
accomplish	*ed, ing, es*
according	*ly*
account	*ed, ing, ant, s*
accumulate	*d, ∮ing, s*
accuracy	
accurate	*ly*
accusation	*s*
accuse	*d, ∮ing, s*
accustom	*ed, ing, s*
ache	*d, ∮ing, s*
achieve	*d, ∮ing, ment, s*
acid	*s*
acknowledge	*d, ∮ing, s*
acknowledg(e)ment	*s*
acorn	*s*
acquaint	*ed, ing, ance, s*
acquire	*d, ∮ing, ment, s*
acre	*age, s*
acrobat	*ic, s*
across	
act	*ed, ing, s*
actor	*s*
actress	*es*
action	*s*
active	*ly*
activity	*ies*
actual	*ly*

*∮ Drop **e** before adding ing*

* accept
   except

ad   ae af ag

ad	
adapt	able, ed, ing, or, s
add	ed, ing, s
addition	al, s
adder	s
address	ed, ing, es
adequate	ly
adhere	d, ∉ing, s
adhesive	s
adjective	s
adjoin	ed, ing, s
adjust	able, ed, ing, ment, s
admirabl e	y
admiral	s
admiration	
admire	d, ∉ing, r, s
admission	s
admit	ted, ting, s
admittance	
adopt	ed, ing, ion, s
adorabl e	y
adore	d, ∉ing, s
adorn	ed, ing, ment, s
adrift	
adult	s
advance	d, ∉ing, ment, s
advantage	s
adventure	d, ∉ing, r, s
adventurous	ly, ness
adverb	s
adversar y	ies
advertise	d, ∉ing, r, s
advertisement	s
advice	
advisable	
advise	d, ∉ing, r, s
advocate	d, ∉ing, s

ae	
aerial	s
aerodrome	s
aeronaut	ic, s
aeroplane	s

af	
affair	s
affect	ed, ing, s
affection	s
affectionate	ly, ness
affix	ed, ing, es
afford	ed, ing, s
afloat	
afraid	
after	
afternoon	s
afterwards	

ag	
again	
against	
age	d, less, -group, s
ageing or aging	
agent	s
aggravate	d, ∉ing, s
aggressive	ly, ness
aghast	
agile	ly
agilit y	ies
agitate	d, ∉ing, s
ago	
agonize	d, ∉ing, s
agon y	ies
agree	able, d, ing, ment, s
agricultur e	al
aground	

∉ Drop **e** before adding *ing*

ai

aid	ed, ing, s
ail* (be ill)	ed, ing, ment, s
aim	ed, ing, less, lessly, s
air*	ed, ing, crew, mail, tight, man, men
air*	gun, field, line, port, way, s
aircraft	-carrier
Airedale	s
air force	s
air y	ier, iest, ily, iness
aisle* (part of a church; gangway)	s

al

alarm	ed, ing, ist, -bell, -clock, s
album	s
alcohol	ism, ic, s
alcove	s
ale* (beer)	s
alert	ed, ing, ly, ness, s
algebra	
alibi	s
alien	s
alight	ed, ing, s
alike	
alive	
all right	
alley	way, s
alligator	s
allot	ted, ting, ment, s
allow	*ed, ing, ance, s
all y	ies
almond	-blossom, -paste, -tree, s
almost	
alone	
along	side
aloud* (loudly)	

alphabet	ical, ically, s
already	
Alsatian	s
also	
altar* (church table)	s
alter* (change)	ed, ing, ation, s
alternate	d, ∉ing, ly, s
alternative	ly, s
although	
altitude	s
altogether	
aluminium	
always	

am

amateur	ish, s
amaze	d, ∉ing, ment, s
amber	
ambition	s
ambitious	ly, ness
amble	d, ∉ing, s
ambulance	man, men, s
ambush	ed, ing, es
amend	ed, ing, ment, s
amiabl e	y
amid or amidst	
amiss	
ammunition	
among or amongst	
amount	ed, ing, s
amphibian	s or amphibia
amphibious	ly
ample	r, st, ness
amplifier	s
amputate	d, ∉ing, s
amuse	d, ∉ing, ment, s

∉ Drop **e** before adding *ing*

*				
	ail	air	aisle	allowed	altar
	ale	heir	isle	aloud	alter

4

an   ap

an		ap	
anaesthetic	s	apart	
ancestor	s	apartment	s
ancestr y	ies	ape	d, ǿing, s
anchor	ed, ing, age, s	apiar y	ies
ancient	ly, ness, s	apiece	
anemone	s	apologetic	al, ally
angel	s	apologize	d, ǿing, s
anger	ed, ing, s	apolog y	ies
angr y	ier, iest, ily	apostle	s
angle	d, ǿing, r, s	appal	led, ling, lingly, s
anguish	ed, ing, es	apparatus	es or **apparatus**
animal	s	apparent	ly
ankle	s	appeal	ed, ing, ingly, s
anniversar y	ies	appear	ed, ing, ance, s
announce	d, ǿing, r, ment, s	appendicitis	
annoy	ed, ing, ance, s	appetite	s
annual	ly, s	appetizing	ly
anoint	ed, ing, ment, s	applaud	ed, ing, s
anonymous	ly	applause	
anorak	s	apple	-core, -pie, -sauce, -tart, -tree, s
another		appliance	s
answer	ed, ing, s	applicant	s
ant	-eater, -hill, s	application	s
antarctic		apply	ing
antelope	s	appl ied	ies
antic	s	appoint	ed, ing, ment, s
anticipate	d, ǿing, s	appreciate	d, ǿing, s
anticipation	s	appreciation	
antique	-dealer, -shop, s	apprentice	d, ǿing, ship, s
antirrhinum	s	approach	ed, ing, es
antiseptic	s	approval	
antler	s	approve	d, ǿing, s
anvil	s	approximate	ly, d, ǿing, s
anxiet y	ies	apricot	s
anxious	ly	April	-fool, s
any	body, one, how, thing, way, where	apron	s

ǿ Drop **e** before adding *ing*

aq ar   as

aq

aquarium	s or **aquaria**
aquatic	s
aqueduct	s

ar

arable	
arc* (curve)	-lamp, -light, s
arcade	s
arch	ed, ing, es
archway	s
archaeological	ly
archaeologist	s
archaeology	
archer	y, s
architect	ure, ural, s
arctic	
are	
aren't (are not)	
area	s
arena	s
argue	d, ẹing, s
argument	ative, s
arise	n, ẹing, s
arithmetic	al
ark* (boat; box)	s
arm	ed, ing, band, chair, ful, hole, pit, s
armada	s
armament	s
armistice	s
armour	ed, y, -plated, -plating
arm y	ies
arose	
around	
arouse	d, ẹing, s
arrange	d, ẹing, r, ment, s

array	ed, ing, s
arrest	ed, ing, s
arrival	s
arrive	d, ẹing, s
arrow	-head, s
arsenic	
art	work, s
artist	ic, ically, s
artful	ly, ness
arter y	ies
article	s
artificial	ity, ly, ness
artillery	man, men

as

ascend	ed, ing, s
ascent	s
ascertain	ed, ing, s
ash	en, y, es
ashamed	
ashore	
aside	
ask	ed, ing, s
asleep	
asparagus	
asphyxiate	d, ẹing, s
aspirin	s
ass	es
assail	ed, ing, ant, s
assassin	ation, s
assassinate	d, ẹing, s
assault	ed, ing, s
assemble	d, ẹing, s
assembl y	ies
assist	ed, ing, ance, s
assistant	s

ẹ Drop **e** before adding *ing*

* arc
  ark

at

associate	d, ǿing, s
association	s
assort	ed, ing, ment, s
assume	d, ǿing, s
assure	d, ǿing, s
aster	s
asthma	tic, tical
astonish	ed, ing, es, ment
astound	ed, ing, s
astray	
astride	
astrologer	s
astrolog y	ical
astronaut	s
astronomer	s
astronom y	ical
asylum	s

at

ate* (eat)	
athlete	s
athletic	ally, s
Atlantic	
atlas	es
atmosphere	s
atom	ic, -bomb, s
atrocious	ly, ness
attach	ed, ing, able, es
attachment	s
attack	ed, ing, er, s
attain	ed, ing, able, ment, s
attempt	ed, ing, s
attend	ed, ing, ance, s
attendant	s
attention	s
attentive	ly, ness

au av

attic	s
attitude	s
attract	ed, ing, ion, s
attractive	ly, ness
attribute	d, ǿing, s

au

auburn	
auction	ed, ing, eer, s
audible	
audience	s
audition	ed, ing, s
August	s
aunt	s
auntie s or aunt y	ies
author	s
authoress	es
authorit y	ies
authorize	d, ǿing, s
autobiograph y	ical, ies
autograph	ed, ing, s
automatic	ally
automation	
autumn	al, s

av

available	
avalanche	s
avenge	d, ǿing, r, s
avenue	s
average	d, ǿing, s
aviar y	ies
aviation	
aviator	s
avoid	ed, ing, able, ance, s

ǿ Drop **e** before adding *ing*

* ate
eight (8)

aw

await	ed, ing, s
awake	d, ∉ing, s
awaken	ed, ing, s
award	ed, ing, s
aware	ness
away	
awe	some, struck, stricken
awful	ly, ness
awhile	
awkward	ly, ness
awning	s
awoke or awaked	
awry	

ax

axe	d, ∉ing, -blade, -handle, s
ax is	es
axle	s

ba

babe	s
baboon	s
bab y	ies
bachelor	s
back	ed, ing, cloth, ground, yard, s
backward	ly, ness, s
bacon	
bad	-tempered, ly, ness
badge	s
badger	ed, ing, s
badminton	-racket
baffle	d, ∉ing, s
bag	ged, ging, ful, -snatcher, s
baggage	

bagg y	ier, iest, ily, iness
bagpipe	s
bail* (wicket cross-piece)	s
bait	ed, ing, s
bake	d, ∉ing, r, house, s
baker y	ies
balance	d, ∉ing, r, s
balcony	ies
bald	ing, er, est, ly, ness, -headed
bale* (bundle)	d, ∉ing, r, s
bale* { out of plane or }	d, ∉ing, r, s
bail* { throw out water }	ed, ing, er, s
ball*	-game, point, -pen, room, s
ballast	
ballerina	s
ballet	-dancing, -dancer, -shoe, s
balloon	ed, ing, ist, s
ballot	ed, ing, -paper, s
bamboo	s
ban	ned, ning, s
banana	s
band	ed, ing, sman, smen, stand, s
bandage	d, ∉ing, s
bandit	s
bang	ed, ing, er, s
bangle	s
banish	ed, ing, es, ment
banister	s
banjo	es or s
bank	ed, ing, er, -book, note, s
bankrupt	ed, ing, s, cy
banner	s
banquet	ed, ing, s
bantam	s
baptism	s
baptize	d, ∉ing, s
bar	red, ring, maid, s

∉ Drop **e** before adding *ing*

* bail	ball
bale	bawl

8

be

barbecue	*d, øing, s*
barbed	*-wire*
barber	*s*
bare* (naked; empty)	*ly, ness, d, øing, s*
bargain	*ed, ing, er, s*
barge	*d, øing, e, -pole, s*
bark	*ed, ing, er, s*
barley	*corn, -sugar, -water, s*
barn	*-dance, -owl, yard, s*
barnacle	*s*
barometer	*s*
baron* (lord)	*et, s*
barrack	*ed, ing, er, -room, -square, s*
barrel	*ful, s*
barren* (bare; empty)	*ly, ness*
barricade	*d, øing, s*
barrier	*s*
barrister	*s*
barrow	*-boy, s*
barter	*ed, ing, er, s*
base	*d, øing, r, st, ly, less, ness, -line, s*
baseball	*s*
basement	*s*
bash	*ed, ing, es*
bashful	*ly, ness*
basin	*ful, s*
bask	*ed, ing, s*
basket	*ball, ful, s*
bat	*ted, ting, sman, smen, s*
batch	*es*
bath	*ed, ing, mat, robe, room, -water, s*
bathe	*d, øing, r, s*
bathing-costume	*s*
baton	*s*
battalion	*s*
batter	*ed, ing, s*
batter *y*	*ies*

battle	*d, øing, axe, field, ship, s*
bawl* (shout; cry out)	*ed, ing, s*
bay	*-window, s*
bayonet	*ed, ing, s*
bazaar	*s*

be

beach* (seashore)	*ed, ing, es*
beacon	*s*
bead	*ed, ing, work, s*
beak	*s*
beaker	*s*
beam	*ed, ing, s*
bean* (plant)	*-bag, pole, stalk, s*
bear* (carry; endure)	*able, ing, er, s*
bear* (animal)	*skin, s*
beard	*ed, s*
beast	*s*
beastl *y*	*ier, iest, iness*
beat* (hit; defeat)	*en, ing, er, s*
beautiful	*ly*
beaut *y*	*ies*
beaver	*s*
became	
because	
beckon	*ed, ing, s*
become	*øing, s*
bed	*ded, ding, clothes, side, time, room, s*
bee	*hive, line, keeper, s*
beech* (tree)	*es*
beef	*burger, eater, steak, s*
been* (past of be)	
beer	*y, -barrel, -bottle, -can, s*
beet* (vegetable)	*root, s*
beetle	*s*
before	*hand*

*ø Drop **e** before adding ing*

*	bare	baron		bawl	beach	bean	beat
	bear	barren		ball	beech	been	beet

bi

beg	ged, ging, s
beggar	ly, s
began	
begin	ning, ner, s
begun	
begone	
behave	d, ∅ing, s
behaviour	
behead	ed, ing, s
behind	hand
being	s
belief	s
believe	d, ∅ing, r, s
bell	-ringer, -tent, -tower, s
bellow	ed, ing, er, s
belong	ed, ing, s
below	
belt	ed, ing, s
bench	es
bend	ing, er, s
bent	
beneath	
benefit	ed, ing, s
benevolent	ly
beret* (cap)	s
berry* (fruit)	ies
berth* (bunk; moor a ship)	ed, ing, s
beside	s
besiege	d, ∅ing, r, s
best	-seller
bet	ted, ting, ter, s
betray	al, ed, ing, er, s
better	ed, ing, s
between	
beware	
bewilder	ed, ing, ment, s
beyond	

bi

Bible	s
bicker	ed, ing, s
bicycle	d, ∅ing, -clip, -pump, s
bid	ding, der, s
bide	d, ∅ing, s
big	ger, gest, ness
bike	d, ∅ing, s
bikini	s
bilberry	ies
bilge	-water, -pump, s
bilious	ly, ness
bill	ed, ing, s
billet	ed, ing, s
billiard	-ball, -cue, -room, -table, s
billion	s
billow	ed, ing, s
bind	ing, er, s
bingo	-hall, s
binoculars	
biography	ical, ies
biology	ical, ist
biped	s
birch	es
bird	-bath, -cage, -seed, -table, s
birth* (born)	day, mark, place, rate, s
biscuit	s
bisect	ed, ing, ion, s
bishop	s
bison	bison
bit	ty, s
bitch	es
bite	∅ing, r, s
bitten	
bitter	er, est, ly, ness
bittern	s
bivouac	ked, king, s

∅ Drop **e** before adding *ing*

* beret berth
  berry birth
  bury

10

bl

bo

bl

black	*ed, ing, er, est, ness, smith, s*
black	*-beetle, bird, board, -currant, s*
blackberry	*ing*
blackberr *ied*	*ies*
blacken	*ed, ing, s*
blackmail	*ed, ing, er, s*
blade	*d, s*
blame	*d, ǿing, less, s*
blancmange	*s*
blank	*ed, ing, er, est, ly, ness, s*
blanket	*s*
blare	*d, ǿing, s*
blast	*ed, ing, s*
blaze	*d, ǿing, s*
blazer	*s*
bleach	*ed, ing, es*
bleak	*er, est, ly, ness*
bleat	*ed, ing, s*
bleed	*ing, s*
bled	
blend	*ed, ing, er, s*
bless	*ed, ing, ings, es*
blew* (blow)	
blind	*ed, ing, er, est, ly, ness, s*
blindfold	*ed, ing, s*
blind-man's-buff	
blink	*ed, ing, er, s*
blister	*ed, ing, s*
blizzard	*s*
block	*age, ed, ing, s*
blockade	*d, ǿing, s*
blond (masc.)	*er, est, s*
blonde (fem.)	*r, st, s*
blood	*hound, shed, -stained, thirsty, y*
bloom	*ed, ing, s*
blossom	*ed, ing, s*

blot	*ted, ting, ter, s*
blouse	*s*
blow	*n, ing, y, er, lamp, pipe, s*
blue* (colour)	*r, st, ness, bell, bottle, s*
blunder	*ed, ing, s*
blunt	*ed, ing, er, est, ly, ness, s*
blush	*ed, ing, es*
bluster	*ed, ing, y, s*

bo

boar* (male pig)	*s*
board* (wood; ship; lodge)	*ed, ing, s*
boarder* (one who boards; lodger)	*s*
boast	*ed, ing, er, s*
boastful	*ly, ness*
boat	*ed, ing, er, man, men, -race, s*
bob	*bed, bing, -sleigh, s*
bod *y*	*ies*
bog	*ged, ging, s*
bogg *y*	*ier, iest, iness*
boil	*ed, ing, er, s*
boisterous	*ly, ness*
bold	*er,* est, ly, ness*
bolt	*ed, ing, s*
bomb	*ed, ing, er, -proof, shell, sight, s*
bombard	*ed, ing, ment, s*
bone	*d, ǿing, ǿy, -dry, -idle, -shaker, s*
bonfire	*s*
bonnet	*s*
bonn *y*	*ier, iest, ily, iness*
book	*ed, ing, case, let, seller, stall, s*
booking office	*s*
boom	*ed, ing, s*
boot	*ed, ing, lace, s*
border* (edge)	*ed, ing, er, less, line, s*
bore* (drill hole; weary)	*d,* ǿing, dom, s*

ǿ Drop **e** before adding *ing*

*	blew	boar	board	boarder	bolder
	blue	bore	bored	border	boulder

br_a

born* (birth)	
borne* (carried)	
borrow	*ed, ing, er, s*
boss	*ed, ing, es*
boss *y*	*ier, iest, ily, iness*
botan *y*	*ical, ist*
both	
bother	*ed, ing, some, s*
bottle	*d, ∅ing, -opener, s*
bottom	*ed, ing, less, s*
bough* (branch)	*s*
bought (buy)	
boulder* (large rock)	*s*
bounce	*d, ∅ing, r, s*
bound	*ed, ing, less, s*
boundar *y*	*ies*
bouquet	*s*
bow* (bend)	*ed, ing, s*
bow	*man, men, shot, string, -tie, s*
bowl	*ed, ing, er, s*
bowl	*ful, s*
box	*ed, ing, es*
boxer	*s*
Boxing Day	*s*
boy* (lad)	*ish, hood, -friend, s*
Boy Scout	*s*

br

brace	*d, ∅ing, s*
bracelet	*s*
bracken	
bracket	*ed, ing, s*
brag	*ged, ging, gart, s*
braid	*ed, ing, s*
brain	*ed, ing, less, storm, wave, s*
brain *y*	*ier, iest, ily, iness*

brake* (to stop)	*d, ∅ing, s*
bramble	*s*
branch	*ed, ing, es*
brand	*ed, ing, -new, s*
brandish	*ed, ing, es*
brand *y*	*ies*
brass	*es*
brave	*d, ∅ing, r, st, ly, s*
bravery	
bravo	*s*
brawl	*ed, ing, er, s*
brawn	
brawn *y*	*ier, iest, iness*
brazen	*ed, ing, ly, ness*
brazier	*s*
bread*	*-bin, -board, -sauce, -crumb, s*
breadth	*s*
break*	*able, age, ing, er, -down, water, s*
breakfast	*ed, ing, -table, -room, s*
breast	*ed, ing, plate, -stroke, s*
breath	*less, lessly, -taking, s*
breathe	*d, ∅ing, r, s*
bred* (brought-up)	
breed	*ing, er, s*
breeze	*s*
breez *y*	*ier, iest, ily, iness*
brew	*ed, ing, er, s*
brewer *y*	*ies*
bribe	*d, ∅ing, ry, s*
brick	*ed, ing, laying, layer, work, yard, s*
bridal* (of a bride, wedding)	*-gown*
bride	*groom, smaid, s*
bridge	*d, ∅ing, head, s*
bridle* (horse's headgear)	*-path, road, s*
brief	*ed, ing, er, est, ly, ness, case, s*
brigade	*s*
brigand	*s*

*∅ Drop **e** before adding ing*

*	born	bough	boulder	boy	brake	bread	bridal
	borne	bow	bolder	buoy	break	bred	bridle

bright	*er, est, ly, ness*
brighten	*ed, ing, s*
brilliance	
brilliant	*ly*
brim	*med, ming, ful, s*
bring	*ing, s*
brink	*s*
brisk	*er, est, ly, ness*
bristle	*d, ∉ing, s*
bristl *y*	*ier, iest, iness*
brittle	*ness*
broad	*er, est, ly, -minded, side, s*
broaden	*ed, ing, s*
broadcast	*ing, er, s*
brocade	*s*
broccoli	
broke	
broken	*-down, -hearted*
bronchitis	
bronze	*d, ∉ing, s*
brooch	*es*
brood	*ed, ing, y, s*
brook	*s*
broom	*stick, s*
broth	*s*
brother	*ly, s*
brother(*s*)**-in-law**	
brought (bring)	
brow	*s*
brown	*ed, ing, er, est, ish, ness, s*
brownie	*s*
bruise	*d, ∉ing, r, s*
brunette	*s*
brush	*ed, ing, es*
Brussels sprouts	
brutal	*ity, ly*
brute	*s*

bu

bubble	*d, ∉ing, -bath, -gum, s*
bubbl *y*	*ier, iest, iness*
buccaneer	*s*
buck	*ed, ing, skin, s*
bucket	*ful, s*
buckle	*d, ∉ing, s*
bud	*ded, ding, s*
budge	*d, ∉ing, s*
budgerigar	*s*
budget	*ed, ing, s*
buffalo	*es* or **buffalo**
buffer	*s*
buffet	*ed, ing, s*
bugle	*-call, r, s*
build	*ing, er, s*
built	
bulb	*s*
bulge	*d, ∉ing, s*
bulk	
bulk *y*	*ier, iest, ily, iness*
bull	*dog, fight, frog, ring, -terrier, s*
bull's-eye	*s*
bulldoze	*d, ∉ing, r, s*
bullet	*-hole, -proof, -wound, s*
bulletin	*s*
bullion	
bullock	*s*
bully	*ing*
bull *ied*	*ies*
bulrush	*es*
bumble-bee	*s*
bump	*ed, ing, er, s*
bump *y*	*ier, iest, ily, iness*
bunch	*ed, ing, es*
bundle	*d, ∉ing, s*
bung	*ed, ing, -hole, s*

∉ Drop **e** before adding *ing*

bungalow	s
bungle	d, ᴇ́ing, r, s
bunk	s
bunker	ed, ing, s
Bunsen burner	s
bunting	
buoy* (floating marker)	ant, ed, ing, s
burden	ed, ing, some, s
bureau	x or s
burglar	-alarm, s
burglar y	ies
burgle	d, ᴇ́ing, s
burial	-ground, -place, s
burl y	ier, iest, ily, iness
burn	ed, ing, er, s
burnt or **burned**	
burrow	ed, ing, er, s
burst	ing, s
bury* (cover)	ing
bur ied	ies
bus	man, men, es
busb y	ies
bush	es
bush y	ier, iest, ily, iness
business	man, men, es
bustle	d, ᴇ́ing, r, s
busy	ing, ness
bus ied	ier, iest, ily, ies
butcher	ed, ing, s
butler	s
butter	ed, ing, scotch, cup, s
butterfl y	ies
button	ed, ing, -hole, s
buy* (purchase)	ing, er, s
buzz	ed, ing, es
buzzer	s
buzzard	s

by

by* (near to, etc.)	
bye* (a run)	s
bygone	s
by-pass	ed, ing, es
bystander	s
byway	s

ca

cabaret	s
cabbage	s
cabin	-boy, s
cabinet	-maker, s
cable	d, ᴇ́ing, gram, -car, s
cackle	d, ᴇ́ing, r, s
cactus	es or **cacti**
caddie* (golfer's club-carrier)	d, s
caddying	
cadd y* (tea box)	ies
cadet	s
cadge	d, ᴇ́ing, r, s
café	s
cafeteria	s
cage	d, ᴇ́ing, s
cake	d, ᴇ́ing, s
calamit y	ies
calculate	d, ᴇ́ing, s
calculation	s
calculator	s
calendar	s
calf	skin, **calves**
call	ed, ing, er, s
calm	ed, ing, er, est, ly, ness, s
came	
camel	-hair, s
camera	man, men, s
camouflage	d, ᴇ́ing, s

ᴇ́ Drop **e** before adding *ing*

*	buoy	bury	buy	caddie
	boy	beret	bye	caddy
		berry	by	

14

camp	*ed, ing, er, -bed, -fire, site, s*	**career**	*ed, ing, s*
campaign	*ed, ing, er, s*	**caress**	*ed, ing, es*
canal	*s*	**cargo**	*es*
canary	*ies*	**caricature**	*d, ǿing, s*
cancel	*led, ling, lation, s*	**carnation**	*s*
candidate	*s*	**carnival**	*s*
candle	*-light, wick, stick, s*	**carnivorous**	
candy	*ied, ies*	**carol**	*led, ling, ler, -singer, s*
cane	*d, ǿing, s*	**carpenter**	*s*
cannibal	*ism, s*	**carpentry**	
cannon	*ed, -ball, -shot, s* or **cannon**	**carpet**	*ed, ing, -sweeper, s*
cannot		**carriage**	*way, s*
can't (cannot)		**carrot**	*s*
canoe	*d, ing, ist, s*	**carry**	*ing*
canteen	*s*	**carr**ied	*ies*
canter	*ed, ing, s*	**carrier**	*-bag, -pigeon, s*
canvas* (strong cloth)	*es*	**cart**	*ed, ing, -load, -horse, -wheel, s*
canvass* (seek votes, orders)	*ed, ing, es*	**carton**	*s*
canyon	*s*	**cartoon**	*ed, ing, ist, s*
capable	*y*	**cartridge**	*-belt, -case, s*
cape	*s*	**carve**	*d, ǿing, r, s*
capital	*s*	**cascade**	*d, ǿing, s*
capsize	*d, ǿing, s*	**case**	*s*
capsule	*s*	**cash**	*ed, ing, -box, es*
captain	*ed, ing, s*	**cashier**	*s*
captive	*s*	**cask**	*s*
captivity	*ies*	**casket**	*s*
capture	*d, ǿing, s*	**casserole**	*d, ǿing, s*
car	*-load, -park, port, s*	**cassette**	*-player, -recorder, s*
caramel	*s*	**cast**	*ing, s*
caravan	*ned, ning, ner, s*	**castaway**	*s*
carcasses or **carcase**	*s*	**castle**	*s*
card	*board, -game, -room, -table, s*	**castor oil**	
cardigan	*s*	**casual**	*ly, ness, s*
care	*d, ǿing, free, taker, s*	**casualt**y	*ies*
careful	*ly, ness*	**catalogue**	*d, ǿing, s*
careless	*ly, ness*	**catapult**	*ed, ing, s*

ǿ Drop **e** before adding *ing*

* canvas
canvass

ce

catastrophe	s
catch	ing, es
catch y	ier, iest, iness
cater	ed, ing, er, s
caterpillar	s
cathedral	s
Catherine wheel	s
Catholic	s
catkin	s
cattle	-market, -shed, -show, -truck
caught	
cauldron	s
cauliflower	s
cause	d, ǿing, s
caution	ed, ing, s
cautious	ly, ness
cavalier	s
cavalry	
cave	d, ǿing, -man, -men, -dweller, s
cavern	s
cavit y	ies

ce

cease	d, ǿing, less, lessly, s
cedar	s
ceiling* (roof of room)	s
celandine	s
celebrate	d, ǿing, s
celebration	s
celebrit y	ies
celery	
cell* (small room)	s
cellar* (underground room)	s
cello	s
cellophane	
cement	ed, ing, -mixer, s

cha

cemeter y	ies
cent* (coin)	s
centigrade	
centimetre	s
central	ly
centre	d, ǿing, -forward, -piece, s
centur y	ies
cereal* (wheat, oats, etc.)	s
ceremon y	ies
certain	ly, ty
certificate	s

ch

chaffinch	es
chain	ed, ing, -mail, -saw, -store, s
chair	ed, ing, man, woman, -lift, s
chalet	s
chalk	ed, ing, s
chalk y	ier, iest, iness
challenge	d, ǿing, r, s
chamber	maid, s
chamois	-leather
champagne	s
champion	ed, ing, ship, s
chance	d, ǿing, s
chandelier	s
change	able, d, ǿing, s
channel	led, ling, s
chant	ed, ing, s
chaos	
chaotic	ally
chapel	s
chapter	s
char	red, ring, woman, women, s
character	istic, s
charade	s

ǿ Drop e before adding ing

*	ceiling	cell	cellar	cent	cereal
	sealing	sell	seller	sent	serial
				scent	

charcoal		**chick**	*weed, s*	
charge	*d, e̸ing, r, s*	**chicken**	*-feed, -wire, s* or **chicken**	
chariot	*eer, s*	**chicken-pox**		
charit *y*	*ies*	**chief**	*ly, tain, s*	
charm	*ed, ing, er, s*	**chilblain**	*s*	
chart	*ed, ing, room, s*	**child**	*ish, hood, like, less,* **children**	
charter	*ed, ing, s*	**chill**	*ed, ing, er, s*	
chase	*d, e̸ing, r, s*	**chill** *y*	*ier, iest, ily, iness*	
chasm	*s*	**chime**	*d, e̸ing, s*	
chat	*ted, ting, s*	**chimney**	*-pot. -stack, -sweep, s*	
chatter	*ed, ing, er, s*	**chimpanzee**	*s*	
chatt *y*	*ier, iest, ily, iness*	**chin**	*-strap, s*	
chauffeur	*s*	**china**	*-shop, ware*	
cheap	*er, est, ly, ness*	**chink**	*ed, ing, s*	
cheapen	*ed, ing, s*	**chintz**	*es*	
cheat	*ed, ing, er, s*	**chip**	*ped, ping, per, s*	
check*	*ed, ing, er, -list, -out, -point, s*	**chirp**	*ed, ing, s*	
check* (pattern)	*ed, s*	**chirp** *y*	*ier, iest, ily, iness*	
cheek	*ed, ing, -bone, s*	**chisel**	*led, ling, s*	
cheek *y*	*ier, iest, ily, iness*	**chivalrous**	*ly*	
cheer	*ed, ing, -leader, s*	**chivalry**		
cheerful	*ly, ness*	**chlorine**		
cheerless	*ly, ness*	**chloroform**	*ed, ing, s*	
cheer *y*	*ier, iest, ily, iness*	**chocolate**	*s*	
cheese	*burger, cake, cloth, -straw, s*	**choice**	*r, st, ly, ness, s*	
chef	*s*	**choir*** (of singers)	*-boy, -master, s*	
chemical	*ly, s*	**choke**	*d, e̸ing, s*	
chemist	*s*	**choose**	*e̸ing, s*	
chemistry		**chose**	*n*	
cheque* (money-order)	*-book, s*	**chop**	*ped, ping, per, s*	
cherish	*ed, ing, es*	**chopstick**	*s*	
cherr *y*	*ies*	**chorus**	*ed, ing, es*	
chess	*-board, -piece, -man, -men*	**chow**	*, s*	
chest	*s*	**christen**	*ed, ing, s*	
chestnut	*-tree, s*	**Christ**		
chew	*ed, ing, y, er, s*	**Christian**	*ity, s*	
chewing-gum		**Christmas**	*-box, es, -time, -tree, sy*	

e̸ Drop **e** before adding *ing*

*	check	choir
	cheque	quire

chromium	*-plated, -plating*
chrysalis	*es*
chrysanthemum	*s*
chubb *y*	*ier, iest, ily, iness*
chuckle	*d, ∅ing, s*
chug	*ged, ging, s*
chum	*med, ming, s*
chumm *y*	*ier, iest, ily, iness*
chunk	*s*
church	*es*
churchyard	*s*
churn	*ed, ing, s*
chute* (a slide)	*s*
chutney	*s*

ci

cider or **cyder**	*s*
cigar	*-case, -holder, -lighter, s*
cigarette	*-case, -holder, -lighter, s*
cinder	*-path, -track, s*
cine-	*camera, film, projector*
cinema	*-goer, s*
circle	*d, ∅ing, s*
circular	*s*
circulate	*d, ∅ing, s*
circulation	*s*
circumference	*s*
circumstance	*s*
circus	*es*
cistern	*s*
citizen	*s*
cit *y*	*ies*
civil	*ity, ly*
civilian	*s*
civilization	*s*
civilize	*d, ∅ing, s*

cl

claim	*ed, ing, s*
clamber	*ed, ing, s*
clamm *y*	*ier, iest, ily, iness*
clamp	*ed, ing, s*
clang	*ed, ing, s*
clank	*ed, ing, s*
clap	*ped, ping, per, s*
clash	*ed, ing, es*
clasp	*ed, ing, s*
class	*ed, ing, es, rooms*
classic	*al, s*
clatter	*ed, ing, s*
claw	*ed, ing, s*
clay	*ey, -pigeon, -pipe, -pit, s*
clean	*ed, ing, er, est, ly, ness, s*
cleanliness	
cleanse	*d, ∅ing, r, s*
clear	*ed, ing, er, est, ly, ness, s*
clench	*ed, ing, es*
clergy	*man, men*
clerk	*s*
clever	*er, est, ly, ness*
click	*ed, ing, s*
client	*s*
cliff	*-top, s*
climate	*s*
climb	*ed, ing, er, s*
cling	*ing, s*
clinic	*al, ally, s*
clink	*ed, ing, er, s*
clip	*ped, ping, per, s*
cloak	*ed, ing, room, s*
clock	*ed, ing, wise, work, -tower, s*
cloister	*ed, ing, s*
close (shut)	*d, ∅ing, s*
close (near; stuffy)	*r, st, ly, ness*

∅ Drop **e** before adding *ing*

* chute
shoot

COa   cob   coc   cod   cof   coi   col   com

cloth *s*	**code** *d, ẹing, s*
clothe *d, ẹing, s*	**coffee** *-bar, -bean, -cup, -pot, -table, s*
clothes *-basket, -horse, -line, -peg*	**coffin** *s*
cloud *ed, ing, less, lessly, burst, s*	**coil** *ed, ing, s*
cloud *y* *ier, iest, ily, iness*	**coin** *age, ed, ing, s*
clover *s*	**coincide** *d, ẹing, s*
clown *ed, ing, s*	**coincidence** *s*
club *bed, bing, house, room, s*	**cold** *er, est, ish, ly, ness, -storage, s*
cluck *ed,ing, s*	**collapse** *d, ẹing, s*
clue *less, s*	**collapsible**
clump *ed, ing, s*	**collar** *-bone, -stud, s*
clums *y* *ier, iest, ily, iness*	**collect** *ed, ing, ion, or, s*
clung	**college** *s*
cluster *ed, ing, s*	**collide** *d, ẹing, s*
clutch *ed, ing, es*	**collision** *s*
clutter *ed, ing, s*	**collie** *s*
	collier *s*
	collier *y* *ies*
co	**colonel*** (officer) *s*
coach *man, men, ed, ing, es*	**colonize** *d, ẹing, s*
coal *man, men, -mine, -miner, s*	**colon** *y* *ies*
coarse* (rough) *r, st, ly, ness*	**colossal** *ly*
coast *al, ed, ing, line, guard, s*	**colour** *ed, ing, ful, less, -scheme, s*
coat *ed, ing, -hanger, s*	**column** *s*
coax *ed, ing, es*	**comb** *ed, ing, s*
cobble *d, ẹing, r, -stone, s*	**combat** *ed, ing, s*
cobra *s*	**combination** *s*
cobweb *by, s*	**combine** *d, ẹing, -harvester, s*
cock *ed, ing, -fight, pit, tail, s*	**come** *ẹing, s*
cockatoo *s*	**comedian** (masc.) *s*
cockerel *s*	**comedienne** (fem.) *s*
cockle *-shell, s*	**comed** *y* *ies*
cockney *s*	**comet** *s*
cockroach *es*	**comfort** *able, ably, ed, ing, s*
cocoa	**comic** *al, ally, s*
coconut *-matting, -milk, -palm, s*	**command** *ed, ing, er, ment, s*
cocoon *s*	**commemorate** *d, ẹing, s*

ẹ Drop **e** before adding *ing*

*   coarse   colonel
     course   kernel

commence	d, ɇing, ment, s	**conceal**	ed, ing, ment, s
comment	ed, ing, ator, s	**conceit**	ed, edly
commentary	ies	**concentrate**	d, ɇing, s
commerce		**concentration**	
commercial	s	**concern**	ed, ing, s
commission	ed, ing, aire, er, s	**concert**	s
commit	ted, ting, ment, s	**conclude**	d, ɇing, s
committee	-room, s	**conclusion**	s
common	er, est, ly, ness, -room, s	**concrete**	d, ɇing, s
commotion	s	**condemn**	ed, ing, ation, s
communicate	d, ɇing, s	**condition**	ed, ing, er, s
communication	s	**conduct**	ed, ing, or, s
communion		**conductress**	es
community	ies	**conference**	s
compact	s	**confess**	ed, ing, es
companion	ship, s	**confession**	s
company	ies	**confetti**	
comparative	ly, s	**confide**	d, ɇing, s
compare	d, ɇing, s	**confidence**	
comparison	s	**confident**	ial, ially, ly
compartment	s	**confirm**	ed, ing, ation, s
compass	es	**confiscate**	d, ɇing, s
compel	led, ling, s	**confuse**	d, ɇing, s
compete	d, ɇing, s	**confusion**	s
competition	s	**congratulate**	d, ɇing, s
competitor	s	**congratulation**	s
complain	ed, ing, s	**congregate**	d, ɇing, s
complaint	s	**congregation**	s
complete	d, ɇing, ly, ness, s	**conjure**	d, ɇing, s
complexion	s	**conjurer** or **conjuror**	s
complicate	d, ɇing, s	**conker*** (horse-chestnut)	s
compliment	ed, ing, ary, s	**connect**	ed, ing, ion, s
compose	d, ɇing, r, s	**conquer*** (defeat) ed, ing, or, s	
composition	s	**conquest**	s
comprehensive school	s	**conscience**	-smitten, s
computer	s	**conscientious**	ly, ness
comrade	ship, s	**conscious**	ly, ness

ɇ Drop **e** before adding *ing*

* conker
  conquer

20

consent	*ed, ing, s*	**cook**	*ed, ing, er, ery, book, house, s*
consequence	*s*	**cool**	*ed, ing, er, est, ish, ly, ness, s*
consequent	*ly*	**co-operate**	*d, ∉ing, s*
conservative	*s*	**co-operation**	
consider	*ed, ing, able, ably, ate, ation, s*	**copper**	*s*
consist	*ed, ing, s*	**coppice** or **copse**	*s*
consolation	*-prize, s*	**copy**	*ing*
conspicuous	*ly, ness*	**cop** *ied*	*ies*
constable	*s*	**coral**	*-island, -reef, s*
constant	*ly*	**cord**	*s*
construct	*ed, ing, ion, or, s*	**cordial**	*s*
consult	*ed, ing, ation, s*	**cordon**	*ed, ing, s*
consume	*d, ∉ing, r, s*	**corduroy**	*s*
contact	*ed, ing, s*	**core*** (middle of apple, etc.)	*d, ∉ing, s*
contain	*ed, ing, er, s*	**corgi**	*s*
contemporar *y*	*ies*	**cork**	*ed, ing, screw, s*
content	*ed, ing, ment, s*	**corn**	*-cob, field, flake, s*
contest	*ed, ing, ant, s*	**corned beef**	
continent	*al, s*	**corner**	*ed, ing, s*
continual	*ly*	**cornet**	*s*
continue	*d, ∉ing, s*	**coronation**	*s*
continuation		**corporal**	*s*
continuous	*ly, ness*	**corporation**	*s*
contradict	*ed, ing, ion, s*	**corps*** (group of cadets, etc.) **corps**	
contribute	*d, ∉ing, s*	**corpse**	*s*
contribution	*s*	**correct** *ed, ing, ion, ly, ness, s*	
control *led, ling, ler, -column, -lever, s*		**correspond** *ed, ing, ence, ent, s*	
convalesce *d, ∉ing, nce, nt, s*		**corridor**	*s*
convenience	*s*	**cosmetic**	*s*
convenient	*ly*	**cosmonaut**	*s*
convent	*s*	**cost**	*ing, s*
conversation	*s*	**costl** *y*	*ier, iest, iness*
convert	*ed, ing, s*	**coster**	*monger, s*
convey	*ed, ing, ance, s*	**costume**	*s*
convict	*ed, ing, ion, s*	**cos** *y*	*ier, iest, ily, iness, ies*
convince	*d, ∉ing, s*	**cottage**	*s*
convoy	*ed, ing, s*	**cotton**	*wool, s*

∉ Drop **e** before adding *ing*

* core

corps

couch	es
cough	ed, ing, er, -drop, -mixture, s
could	
couldn't (could not)	
council	lor, -chamber, -house, s
count	ed, ing, er, less, -down, s
counter	ed, ing, -attack, foil, s
countess	es
countr y	ies
count y	ies
couple	d, ǿing, s
coupon	s
courage	
courageous	ly, ness
course* (track; direction; of course)	s
court	ed, ing, ier, room, ship, yard, s
courtes y	ies
cousin	ly, s
cove	s
cover	ed, ing, s
cow	boy, hand, herd, hide, shed, s
coward	s
cowardice	
cowardl y	iness
cowslip	s

cr

crab	-apple, -pot, s
crack	ed, ing, er, s
crackle	d, ǿing, s
cradle	d, ǿing, s
craft	sman, smen, s
craft y	ier, iest, ily, iness
cram	med, ming, mer, s
cramp	ed, ing, s
crane	d, ǿing, -driver, s

crank	ed, ing, s
crash	ed, ing, es
crate	d, ǿing, ful, s
crater	s
crave	d, ǿing, s
crawl	ed, ing, er, s
crayon	ed, ing, s
craze	d, ǿing, s
craz y	ier, iest, ily, iness
creak* (noise)	ed, ing, s
creak y	ier, iest, ily, iness
cream	ed, ing, er, -cake, -cheese, s
cream y	ier, iest, ily, iness
crease	d, ǿing, s
create	d, ǿing, s
creature	s
credit	able, ed, ing, or, s
creek* (small bay, sea-coast inlet)	s.
creep	ing, er, s
creep y	ier, iest, ily, iness
cremate	d, ǿing, s
crematorium	s
creosote	d, ǿing, s
crept	
crescent	s
crest	ed, ing, fallen, s
crevice	s
crew	ed, ing, s
crib	bed, bing, ber, s
cricket	ing, er, -field, s
cried	
crier	s
cries	
crime	s
criminal	s
crimson	ed, ing, s
cringe	d, ǿing, s

ǿ Drop **e** before adding *ing*

crinkle	d, ∉ing, s	**crumple**	d, ∉ing, s
crinkly	ier, iest, iness	**crunch**	ed, ing, es
cripple	d, ∉ing, s	**crusade**	d, ∉ing, r, s
crisp	ed, ing, er, est, ly, ness, s	**crush**	ed, ing, es
crispy	ier, iest, ily, iness	**crust**	s
critic	al, ally, ism, s	**crust**y	ier, iest, ily, iness
criticize	d, ∉ing, s	**crutch**	es
croak	ed, ing, er, s	**cry**	ing
croaky	ier, iest, ily, iness	**cr**ied	ies
crochet	ed, ing, -hook, s	**crypt**	s
crockery		**crystal**	s
crocodile	s		
crocus	es		
crook	s		**cu**
crooked	ly, ness	**Cub Scout**	s
crop	ped, ping, per, s	**cube**	d, ∉ing, s
croquet		**cubicle**	s
cross	ed, ing, er, est, ly, ness, es	**cuckoo**	-clock, s
crossroad	s	**cucumber**	s
crossword	s	**cuddle**	d, ∉ing, some, s
crouch	ed, ing, es	**cue*** (hint; billiard-stick)	s
crow	ed, ing, bar, s	**cuff**	-link, s
crowd	ed, ing, s	**cul-de-sac**	**culs-de-sac**
crown	ed, ing, s	**culprit**	s
crucify	ing	**cultivate**	d, ∉ing, s
crucified	ies	**cultivation**	
crucifix	es	**cunning**	ly
crucifixion	s	**cup**	ful, s
crude	r, st, ly, ness	**cupboard**	s
cruel	ler, lest, ly	**curate**	s
cruelty	ies	**curator**	s
cruet	s	**curb*** (hold back)	ed, ing, s
cruise	d, ∉ing, r, s	**curdle**	d, ∉ing, s
crumb	s	**cure**	d, ∉ing, s
crumble	d, ∉ing, s	**curio**	s
crumbly	ier, iest, iness	**curiosit**y	ies
crumpet	s	**curious**	ly, ness

∉ Drop **e** before adding *ing*

cy da

curl	ed, ing, er, s
curl y	ier, iest, ily, iness
currant* (fruit)	-bread, -bun, -cake, s
current* (flow of water, air, etc.)	s
curr y	ied, ies
curse	d, ẹing, s
curt	ly, ness
curtain	ed, ing, s
curtsy	ing
curts ied	ies
curve	d, ẹing, s
cushion	s
custard	-powder, -pie, s
custom	s
customer	s
cut	ting, ter, -price, -rate, -throat, s
cutlass	es
cutlery	

cy

cycle	d, ẹing, -clip, s
cyclist	s
cyclone	s
cygnet* (young swan)	s
cylinder	s
cymbal	ist, s
cypress	es

da

dab	bed, bing, ber, s
dabble	d, ẹing, r, s
dachshund	s
dad	s
dadd y	ies
daffodil	s

daft	er, est, ly, ness
dagger	s
dahlia	s
dail y	ies
daint y	ier, iest, ily, iness, ies
dair y	ies
dais y	ies
dale	s
Dalmatian	s
dam	med, ming, s
damage	d, ẹing, s
dame	s
damp	ed, ing, er, est, ly, ness, s
dampen	ed, ing, er, s
damson	-tree, s
dance	d, ẹing, r, -band, -floor, s
dandelion	s
danger	s
dangerous	ly
dangle	d, ẹing, s
dank	er, est, ly, ness
dapple	d, ẹing, -grey, s
dare	d, ẹing, -devil, s
dark	er, est, ly, ness
darken	ed, ing, s
darling	s
darn	ed, ing, er, s
dart	ed, ing, -board, s
dash	ed, ing, es
date	d, ẹing, -stamp, -palm, s
daub	ed, ing, er, s
daughter	s
dawdle	d, ẹing, r, s
dawn	ed, ing, s
day	break, dream, light, time, s
daze	d, ẹing, s
dazzle	d, ẹing, r, s

ẹ Drop **e** before adding *ing*

*	currant	cygnet
	current	signet

de

dead	-beat, -end, -heat, line, lock, ness
deaden	ed, ing, er, s
deadly	ier, iest, iness
deaf	-aid, er, est, ly, ness
deafen	ed, ing, s
deal	ing, er, s
dealt	
dear* (beloved; costly)	er, est, ly, ness, s
death	ly, -bed, -blow, -rate, -ray, -trap, s
debate	d, ǿing, r, s
debris	
debt	or, s
decay	ed, ing, s
deceit	ful, fully, s
deceive	d, ǿing, r, s
December	s
decent	ly
decide	d, dly, ǿing, s
decimal	s
decipher	ed, ing, s
decision	s
deck	ed, ing, -chair, s
declare	d, ǿing, s
decline	d, ǿing, s
decorate	d, ǿing, s
decoration	s
decorator	s
decrease	d, ǿing, s
deduct	ed, ing, ion, s
deed	s
deep	er, est, ly, ness
deepen	ed, ing, s
deer* (animal)	skin, stalker, -park, **deer**
defeat	ed, ing, s
defect	ive, s
defence	less, lessly, s

defend	ed, ing, er, s
defiant	ly
definite	ly
degree	s
delay	ed, ing, s
deliberate	ly, ness, d, ǿing, s
delicacy	ies
delicate	ly, ness
delicious	ly, ness
delight	ed, ing, s
delightful	ly, ness
deliver	ed, ing, ance, s
delivery	ies
deluge	d, ǿing, s
demand	ed, ing, s
demolish	ed, ing, es
demon	s
demonstrate	d, ǿing, s
demonstration	s
demonstrator	s
dense	r, st, ly, ness
dent	ed, ing, s
dentist	s
deny	ing
denied	ies
depart	ed, ing, ure, s
department	s
depend	ed, ing, able, ent, s
deport	ed, ing, ation, s
deposit	ed, ing, or, s
depot	s
depth	-charge, s
deputy	ies
derail	ed, ing, ment, s
derelict	s
descant	-recorder, s
descend	ed, ing, ant, s

ǿ Drop **e** before adding *ing*

* dear
  deer

di

descent	s
describe	d, ẹing, s
description	s
desert (sandy place)	s
desert* (run away)	ed, ing, ion, er, s
deserve	d, ẹing, s
design	ed, ing, er, s
desire	d, ẹing, s
desk	s
desolate	d, ẹing, ly, ness, s
despair	ed, ing, ingly, s
despatch or **dispatch**	ed, ing, es
desperate	ly, ness
desperation	
despise	d, ẹing, s
despite	
dessert* (fruit, pudding, etc.)	-spoon, s
destination	s
destroy	ed, ing, er, s
destruction	
destructive	ly, ness
detach	ed, ing, es
detail	ed, ing, s
detain	ed, ing, s
detect	ed, ing, ion, or, s
detective	s
detention	s
determination	
determine	d, ẹing, s
detest	able, ed, ing, s
develop	ed, ing, er, ment, s
device	s
devil	ish, ry, ment, s
devise	d, ẹing, s
devote	d, ẹing, s
devour	ed, ing, er, s
dew* (moisture)	y, -drop, -fall, -pond, s

di

diagram	s
dial	led, ling, ler, s
dialect	s
dialogue	s
diameter	s
diamond	s
diary	ies
dictate	d, ẹing, s
dictation	s
dictionary	ies
didn't (did not)	
die* (small spotted cube)	**dice**
die* (lose life)	s
died* (lost life)	
dying* (losing life)	
diet	ed, ing, ician, s
differ	ed, ing, ence, s
different	ly
difficult	
difficulty	ies
dig	ging, ger, s
digest	ed, ing, ion, ive, s
dignify	ied, ies
dignity	
dike or **dyke**	s
dilapidated	
dilute	d, ẹing, s
dim	med, ming, mer, mest, ly, ness, s
dimension	s
dimple	d, ẹing, s
dine	d, ẹing, r, s
dining	-car, -hall, -room, -table
dinghy	ies
dingy	ier, iest, ily, iness
dinner	-hour, -service, -table, -time, s
dinosaur	s

ẹ Drop **e** before adding *ing*

*	desert	dew		die	died	dying
	dessert	due		dye	dyed	dyeing
		Jew				

dip	ped, ping, per, s	**dismal**	ly, ness
diploma	s	**dismantle**	d, ∉ing, s
direct	ed, ing, ly, ness, ive, or, s	**dismay**	ed, ing, s
direction	-finder, s	**dismiss**	ed, ing, es
director y	ies	**dismount**	ed, ing, s
dirt	-track	**disobedience**	
dirt ied	ier, iest, ily, iness, ies	**disobedient**	ly
dirty	ing	**disobey**	ed, ing, s
disable	d, ∉ing, ment, s	**disorder**	ly, s
disadvantage	s	**dispatch** or **despatch**	ed, ing, es
disagree	able, d, ing, ment, s	**dispensar** y	ies
disappear	ed, ing, ance, s	**dispense**	d, ∉ing, r, s
disappoint	ed, ing, ment, s	**display**	ed, ing, s
disarm	ed, ing, ament, s	**displease**	d, ∉ing, s
disarrange	d, ∉ing, ment, s	**dispute**	d, ∉ing, s
disaster	s	**disqualify**	ing
disastrous	ly	**disqualif** ied	ies, ication
disc or **disk**	s	**dissatisfy**	ing
discharge	d, ∉ing, s	**dissatisf** ied	ies, action
disciple	s	**dissolve**	d, ∉ing, s
discipline	d, ∉ing, s	**distance**	s
discontent	ed, edly, ment, s	**distant**	ly
discothèque or **disco**	-club, -dancing, s	**distinct**	ion, ive, ly, ness
discourage	d, ∉ing, ment, s	**distinguish**	able, ed, ing, es
discover	ed, ing, er, s	**distract**	ed, ing, ion, s
discover y	ies	**distress**	ed, ing, es
discuss	ed, ing, es	**disribute**	d, ∉ing, s
discussion	s	**district**	s
disease	d, s	**disturb**	ed, ing, ance, s
disgrace	d, ∉ing, s	**ditch**	ed, ing, es
disgraceful	ly, ness	**divan**	s
disguise	d, ∉ing, s	**dive**	d, ∉ing, r, s
disgust	ed, ing, s	**divert**	ed, ing, s
dish	ed, ing, es	**divide**	d, ∉ing, r, s
dishearten	ed, ing, s	**division**	s
dishonest	ly, y	**divorce**	d, ∉ing, e, s
dislike	able, d, ∉ing, s	**dizz** y	ier, iest, ily, iness

∉ Drop **e** before adding *ing*

do

dr

do

docile	*ly*
dock	*ed, ing, er, yard, s*
doctor	*' s*
document	*ed, ing, s*
dodge	*d, ǿing, r, s*
doe* (female animal)	*s*
does	
doesn't (does not)	
doing	*s*
dole	*d, ǿing, ful, fully, s*
doll	*s*
dollar	*s*
dolphin	*s*
domestic	*ally, s*
domesticate	*d, ǿing, s*
domino	*es*
donate	*d, ǿing, s*
donation	*s*
done	
donkey	*s*
don't (do not)	
doom	*ed, ing, sday, s*
door	*bell, keeper, mat, step, way, s*
dormitor *y*	*ies*
dose	*d, ǿing, s*
dot	*ted, ting, s*
double	*d, ǿing, -jointed, -decker, s*
doubt	*ed, ing, less, er, s*
doubtful	*ly, ness*
dough* (moist flour)	*boy, nut, y*
douse or **dowse**	*d, ǿing, s*
dove	*cote, s*
dowd *y*	*ier, iest, ily, iness*
down	*stairs, hill, fall, pour, ward, s*
doze	*d, ǿing, s*
dozen	*s* or **dozen**

dr

drab	*ber, best, ly, ness*
drag	*ged, ging, -net, s*
dragon	*s*
dragonfl *y*	*ies*
drain	*age, ed, ing, -pipe, s*
drake	*s*
drama	*tic, tist, s*
dramatize	*d, ǿing, s*
drank	
drape	*d, ǿing, s*
draper	*s*
draper *y*	*ies*
drastic	*ally*
draught	*sman, smen, -board, s*
draught *y*	*ier, iest, ily, iness*
draw	*n, ing, er, s*
drawbridge	*s*
drawer	*s*
drawing	*-board, -paper, -pin, -room, s*
dread	*ed, ing, s*
dreadful	*ly, ness*
dream	*ed, ing, land, like, er, s*
dreamt or **dreamed**	
dream *y*	*ier, iest, ily, iness*
drear *y*	*ier, iest, ily, iness*
dredge	*d, ǿing, r, s*
drench	*ed, ing, es*
dress	*ed, ing, es*
dresser	*s*
dressing	*-gown, -case, -room, -table, s*
dressmaker	*s*
drew	
dribble	*d, ǿing, r, s*
drift	*ed, ing, er, s*
drill	*ed, ing, er, s*
drink	*able, ing, er, s*

ǿ Drop **e** before adding *ing*

* doe
   dough

du   dw   dy

drip	ped, ping, s
drive	⌀ing, r, way, s
driven	
drivel	led, ling, ler, s
drizzle	d, ⌀ing, s
drizzl y	ier, iest, iness
dromedar y	ies
drone	d, ⌀ing, s
droop	ed, ing, s
drop	ped, ping, per, let, s
drought	s
drove	
drown	ed, ing, s
drowse	d, ⌀ing, s
drows y	ier, iest, ily, iness
drudgery	
drug	ged, ging, gist, -addict, store, s
drum	med, ming, mer, -major, stick, s
drunk	ard, s
drunken	ly, ness
dry	ing, ness
dr ied	ier, iest, ies
dryer or **drier** (noun)	s
dryly or **drily**	

du

dual* (two; double)	
duchess	es
duck	ed, ing, ling, s
due* (expected; owing)	s
duel* (a fight)	led, ling, list, s
duet	s
duffel or **duffle**	-bag, -coat, s
dug	-out
duke	dom, s
dull	ed, ing, er, est, ish, y, ness, s

duly	
dumb	er, est, ly, ness
dumm y	ies
dump	ed, ing, s
dumpling	s
dunce	s
dungarees	
dungeon	s
duplicate	d, ⌀ing, s
durable	ness
duration	
during	
dusk	
dusk y	ier, iest, ily, iness
dust	ed, ing, man, men, bin, pan, er, s
dust y	ier, iest, ily, iness
dutiful	ly, ness
dut y	ies

dw

dwarf	ed, ing, s or **dwarves**
dwell	ed, ing, er, s
dwelling	-house, -place, s
dwelt or **dwelled**	
dwindle	d, ⌀ing, s

dy

dye* (colour)	r, s
dyed* (coloured)	
dyeing* (colouring)	
dying* (losing life)	
dyke or **dike**	s
dynamic	al, ally, s
dynamite	d, ⌀ing, s
dynamo	s

⌀ Drop **e** before adding *ing*

*	due	dual	
	dew	duel	
	Jew	jewel	

dye	dyed	dyeing
die	died	dying

ea

each	
eager	*ly, ness*
eagle	*t, s*
ear	*ache, -drum, phone, -plug, -ring, s*
earwig	*s*
earl	*dom, s*
earl *y*	*ier, iest, iness*
earn** (be paid)	*ed, ing, er, s*
earnt or **earned**	
earnest	*ly, ness*
earth	*quake, worm, work, s*
earthen	*ware*
ease	*d, ǿing, s*
eas *y*	*ier, iest, ily, iness*
easel	*s*
east	*ern, erly, ward, wards*
Easter	*-egg, s*
eat	*able, en, ing, er s*
eavesdrop	*ped, ping, per, s*

ec

eccentric	*s*
echo	*ed, ing, es*
éclair	*s*
eclipse	*d, ǿing, s*
economic	*al, ally, s*
economize	*d, ǿing, s*
econom *y*	*ies*

ed

eddy	*ing*
edd *ied*	*ies*
edge	*d, ǿing, ways, wise, s*
edible	

edit	*ed, ing, s*
edition	*s*
editor	*ial, s*
educate	*d, ǿing, s*
education	*al, ally, alist, ist*

ee

eel	*s*
eer *ie* or **eer** *y*	*ier, iest, ily, iness*

ef

effect	*ed, ing, s*
effective	*ly, ness*
efficiency	
efficient	*ly*
effig *y*	*ies*
effort	*less, lessly, s*

eg

egg	*-cup, -shell, -spoon, -timer, s*

ei

eiderdown	*s*
either	

el

elaborate	*d, ǿing, ly, ness, s*
elapse	*d, ǿing, s*
elastic	*ally, ity*
elbow	*ed, ing, s*
elder	*ly, s*
eldest	
elect	*ed, ing, ion, or, s*

*ǿ Drop **e** before adding *ing**

*   earn
    urn

em

en

electric	al, ally, s
electrician	s
electricity	
electrocute	d, ei̶ng, s
elegant	ly
elephant	s
elevator	s
elf	in, ish, **elves**
eligible	
eliminate	d, ei̶ng, s
elimination	s
Elizabethan	s
elm	-tree, s
elocution	ist
elope	d, ei̶ng, ment, s
else	where

em

embankment	s
embark	ed, ing, ation, s
embarrass	ed, ing, es
embarrassment	s
emblem	s
embrace	d, ei̶ng, s
embroider	ed, ing, s
embroider y	ies
emerald	s
emerge	d, ei̶ng, s
emergenc y	ies
emigrate	d, ei̶ng, s
emperor	s
empire	s
employ	ed, ing, ment, ee, er, s
empress	es
empty	ing
empt ied	ier, iest, ily, iness, ies

en

enable	d, ei̶ng, s
enamel	led, ling, s
encamp	ed, ing, ment, s
enchant	ed, ing, ment, s
encircle	d, ei̶ng, ment, s
enclose	d, ei̶ng, s
enclosure	s
encore	d, ei̶ng, s
encounter	ed, ing, s
encourage	d, ei̶ng, ment, s
encyclop(a)edia	s
end	ed, ing, less, lessly, s
endanger	ed, ing, s
endeavour	ed, ing, s
endure	d, ei̶ng, s
endurance	s
enem y	ies
energetic	ally
energ y	ies
enforce	d, ei̶ng, ment, s
engage	d, ei̶ng, ment, s
engine	-driver, -room, s
engineer	ed, ing, s
engrave	d, ei̶ng, r, s
engulf	ed, ing, s
enjoy	able, ed, ing, ment, s
enlarge	d, ei̶ng, r, ment, s
enlist	ed, ing, ment, s
enormous	ly, ness
enough	
enquire or **inquire**	d, ei̶ng, r, s
enquir y or **inquir** y	ies
enrage	d, ei̶ng, s
enrol	led, ling, ment, s
entangle	d, ei̶ng, ment, s
enter	ed, ing, s

ei̶ Drop **e** before adding *ing*

enterprise	s
entertain	ed, ing, ment, er, s
enthusiasm	s
enthusiastic	ally
entire	ly, ness
entitle	d, ǿing, ment, s
entrance	s
entr y	ies
envelope	s
envious	ly, ness
environment	al, alist, s
envy	ing
env ied	ies

ep

epidemic	s
epilogue	s
episode	s

eq

equal	led, ling, ly, s
equalize	d, ǿing, r, s
equator	ial
equip	ped, ping, ment, s
equivalent	ly

er

erase	d, ǿing, r, s
erect	ed, ing, ion, s
err	ed, ing, ant, s
errand	s
erratic	ally
error	s
erupt	ed, ing, ion, s

es

escalator	s
escapade	s
escape	d, ǿing, r, s
escort	ed, ing, s
Eskimo	s or es or **Eskimo**
especial	ly
espionage	
esplanade	s
essay	ist, s
essence	s
essential	ly, s
establish	ed, ing, es
establishment	s
estate	s
estimate	d, ǿing, s
estuar y	ies

ev

evacuate	d, ǿing, s
evacuation	s
evade	d, ǿing, s
evaporate	d, ǿing, s
eve	s
even	ed, ing, ly, ness, s
evening	s
event	ful, less, s
eventual	ly
ever	green, lasting, more
every	body, one, thing, where
evict	ed, ing, ion, s
evidence	s
evident	ly
evil	ly, ness, s
evolve	d, ǿing, s
evolution	s

ǿ Drop **e** before adding *ing*

ex

exact	ly, ness
exaggerate	d, ǿing, s
examination	s
examine	d, ǿing, r, s
examiner	s
example	s
exasperate	d, ǿing, s
excavate	d, ǿing, s
excavation	s
exceed	ed, ing, ingly, s
excel	led, ling, s
excellent	ly
except* (leaving out)	ed, ing, s
exception	al, ally, s
excess	ive, ively, es
exchange	d, ǿing, able, s
excitable	
excite	d, dly, ǿing, ment, s
exclaim	ed, ing, s
exclude	d, ǿing, s
exclusive	ly, ness
excursion	s
excuse	d, ǿing, s
execute	d, ǿing, s
execution	er, s
exercise	d, ǿing, s
exert	ed, ing, ion, s
exhaust	ed, ing, ion, ible, ive, -pipe, s
exhibit	ed, ing, or, s
exhibition	s
exile	d, ǿing, s
exist	ed, ing, ence, ent, s
exit	s
expand	ed, ing, s
expanse	s
expansion	s

expect	ed, ing, ant, ation, s
expedition	s
expel	led, ling, s
expense	s
expensive	ly, ness
experience	d, ǿing, s
experiment	ed, ing, al, ally, s
expert	ise, ly, ness, s
expire	d, ǿing, s
explain	ed, ing, s
explanation	s
explode	d, ǿing, s
exploit	s
exploration	s
explore	d, ǿing, r, s
explosion	s
explosive	s
export	ed, ing, er, s
expose	d, ǿing, s
exposure	s
express	ed, ing, es
expression	s
exquisite	ly, ness
extend	ed, ing, s
extension	s
extensive	ly, ness
extent	
exterior	s
extinct	ion
extinguish	ed, ing, es
extra	s
extract	ed, ing, ion, s
extraordinary	ily, iness
extravagance	s
extravagant	ly
extreme	ly, s
extricate	d, ǿing, s

ǿ Drop **e** before adding *ing*

* except
  accept

ey

eye   *d, ball, brow, lid, sight, sore, s*
eyeing or **eying**
eyelash   *es*

fa

fable   *s*
fabulous   *ly, ness*
face *d, ǿing, -cloth, -flannel, s*
fact   *s*
factor *y*   *ies*
fade   *d, ǿing, s*
faggot   *s*
fail   *ed, ing, ure, s*
faint *er, est, ish, ly, ness, ed, ing, s*
fair* *er, est, ish, ly, ness, ground, s*
fair *y*   *ies*
faith   *s*
faithful   *ly, ness*
fake   *d, ǿing, s*
falcon   *er, s*
fall   *en, ing, s*
false   *hood, r, st, ly, ness*
falter   *ed, ing, s*
fame   *d*
familiar   *ity, ly*
famil *y*   *ies*
famine   *s*
famish   *ed, ing, es*
famous   *ly*
fan *ned, ning, ner, -belt, light, tail, s*
fancy   *ing*
fanc *ied, ier, iest, ies, iful, ifully*
fantastic   *ally*
far *ther,* thest, -away, -off, -fetched*
fare* (price of journey; food) *s*

fe

farewell   *s*
farm *ed, ing, er, -house, yard, s*
fascinate   *d, ǿing, s*
fashion   *able, ably, ed, ing, s*
fast   *er, est, ness, ed, ing, s*
fasten   *ed, ing, er, s*
fat   *ted, ter, test, ness, s*
fatten   *ed, ing, s*
fatt *y*   *ier, iest, iness*
fatal   *ly*
fate* (destiny)   *d, ful, s*
father* (parent)   *less, ly, s*
fathom   *ed, ing, s*
fatigue   *d, ǿing, s*
fault *ed, ing, less, lessly, s*
fault *y*   *ier, iest, ily, iness*
favour *able, ably, ed, ing, itism, s*
favourite   *s*
fawn   *ed, ing, s*

fe

fear   *ed, ing, some, s*
fearful   *ly, ness*
fearless   *ly, ness*
feast   *ed, ing, s*
feat* (difficult deed)   *s*
feather *ed, ing, y, -bed, -duster, s*
feature   *d, ǿing, s*
February   *s*
fed
fee   *s*
feeble   *r, st, ness*
feebly
feed   *ing, er, s*
feel   *ing, er, s*
feet* (pl. of foot)

*ǿ Drop **e** before adding* ing

*   fair   farther   fate   feat
    fare   father   fête   feet

fi

feign	*ed, ing, s*
fell	*ed, ing, s*
fellow	*ship, s*
felt	
female	*s*
feminine	*s*
fence	*d, ǿing, r, s*
fend	*ed, ing, er, s*
fern	*s*
ferocious	*ly, ness*
ferocity	
ferret	*ed, ing, er, s*
ferry	*-boat,ˈ ing, man, men*
ferr *ied*	*ies*
fertile	*ly*
fertilize	*d, ǿing, r, s*
fester	*ed, ing, s*
festival	*s*
festive	*ly*
festivit *y*	*ies*
fetch	*ed, ing, es*
fête* (entertainment; festival)	*d, ǿing, s*
feud	*s*
feudal	*ism*
fever	*ish, ishly, s*
few	*er, est*

fi

fiancé* (masc.)	*s*
fiancée* (fem.)	*s*
fibre	*glass, -tip, s*
fiction	*al*
fictitious	*ly, ness*
fiddle	*d, ǿing, r, stick, s*
fidget	*ed, ing, y, s*
field	*ed, ing, sman, smen, er, s*

fiend	*ish, s*
fierce	*r, st, ly, ness*
fier *y*	*ier, iest, ily, iness*
fight	*ing, er, s*
figure	*d, ǿing, s*
file	*d, ǿing, s*
fill	*ed, ing, er, s*
fillet	*ed, ing, s*
film	*ed, ing, -set, -star, -studio, s*
filter	*ed, ing, -bed, -paper, -tip, s*
filth	
filth *y*	*ier, iest, ily, iness*
final	*ly, ist, s*
finch	*es*
find* (found)	*ing, er, s*
fine	*d,* ***** *ǿing, s*
fine	*r, st, ly, ness*
finger	*ed, ing, -mark, -nail, -print, tip, s*
finish	*ed, ing, es*
fiord or **fjord**	*s*
fir*	*-cone, -tree, s*
fire	*d, ǿing, man, men, place, work, s*
fire	*-alarm, -brigade, -engine, -escape, s*
fire	*-drill, -extinguisher, side, -station, s*
firm	*er, est, ly, ness, s*
first	*ly, -aid, -class, -floor, hand, -rate, s*
fish	*ed, ing, -meal, -paste, y, es* or **fish**
fisher	*man, men, s*
fishing	*-boat, -line, -net, -rod, -tackle*
fishmonger	*s*
fist	*s*
fit	*ted, ting, ter, test, ful, ly, ness, ment, s*
fix	*ed, ing, es*
fixture	*s*
fizz	*ed, ing, es*
fizz *y*	*ier, iest, ily, iness*
fizzle	*d, ǿing, s*

ǿ Drop **e** before adding *ing*

*	fête	fiancé	find	fir
	fate	fiancée	fined	fur

fl

flag	ged, ging, -day, -pole, -staff, s
flagon	s
flake	d, e̸ing, s
flame	d, e̸ing, -thrower, s
flamingo	es or s
flan	s
flank	ed, ing, s
flannel	s
flap	ped, ping, per, jack, s
flare	d, e̸ing, s
flash	ed, ing, es
flash y	ier, iest, ily, iness
flask	s
flat	ter, test, ly, ness, let, s
flatten	ed, ing, s
flatter	ed, ing, y, er, s
flavour	ed, ing, less, s
flaw	ed, less, s
flea* (insect)	-bite, -bitten, s
fleck	ed, ing, s
fledg(e)ling	s
fled	
flee* (run away)	ing, s
fleece	d, e̸ing, s
fleec y	ier, iest, ily, iness
fleet	ing, er, est, ly, ness, s
flesh	-coloured, -wound
flew* (fly)	
flex	ible, ibility, ed, ing, es
flick	ed, ing, s
flicker	ed, ing, s
flier or **flyer**	s
flight	-deck, -recorder, -test, s
flims y	ier, iest, ily, iness
flinch	ed, ing, es
fling	ing, s
flint	lock, stone, s
flint y	ier, iest, ily, iness
flip	ped, ping, per, s
flirt	ed, ing, ation, s
flit	ted, ting, s
float	ed, ing, er, s
flock	ed, ing, s
flog	ged, ging, s
flood	ed, ing, gate, lit, -lighting, -light, s
floor	ed, ing, -board, -cloth, -show, s
flop	ped, ping, s
flopp y	ier, iest, ily, iness
floral	ly
florist	s
flounder	ed, ing, s
flour* (ground wheat)	ed, ing, y, s
flourish	ed, ing, es
flow	ed, ing, s
flower*	ed, ing, y, -bed, -garden, -pot, s
flown	
flu* (influenza)	
flue* (chimney-pipe)	-pipe, s
fluent	ly
fluff	ed, ing, s
fluff y	ier, iest, ily, iness
fluid	s
fluke	d, e̸ing, s
flung	
flurry	ing
flurr ied	ies
flush	ed, ing, es
fluster	ed, ing, s
flute	-player, s
flutter	ed, ing, s
fl y	ies
flyer or **flier**	s
flying	-fish, -machine, -saucer, -squad

e̸ Drop **e** before adding *ing*

* flea flew flour
flee flue flower
flu

fo

fo		**forever**	*more*
foal	*ed, ing, s*	**forfeit**	*ed, ing, ure, s*
foam	*ed, ing, -rubber, s*	**forgave**	
foam *y*	*ier, iest, iness*	**forge**	*d, ǿing, r, s*
fo'c'sle or **forecastle**	*s*	**forger** *y*	*ies*
focus	*ed, ing, es* or **foci**	**forget**	*ting, -me-not, s*
foe	*s*	**forgetful**	*ly, ness*
fog	*ged, ging, -horn, -lamp, -signal, s*	**forgot**	*ten*
fogg *y*	*ier, iest, ily, iness*	**forgive**	*n, ǿing, ness, s*
foil	*ed, ing, s*	**fork**	*ed, ing, s*
fold	*ed, ing, er, s*	**forlorn**	*ly, ness*
foliage		**form**	*ed, ing, ation, s*
folk	*-dance, lore, -song, -tale, s* or **folk**	**former**	*ly*
follow	*ed, ing, er, s*	**formidable**	
foll *y*	*ies*	**formula**	*e* or *s*
fond	*er, est, ly, ness*	**fort*** (castle)	*s*
fondle	*d, ǿing, s*	**forth*** (forward)	*coming*
food	*stuff, store, s*	**fortification**	*s*
fool	*ed, ing, hardy, s*	**fortify**	*ing*
foolish	*ly, ness*	**fortif** *ied*	*ies*
foot	*ing, hold, path, sore, work,* **feet**	**fortnight**	*ly*
football	*er, s*	**fortress**	*es*
footprint	*s*	**fortunate**	*ly*
footstep	*s*	**fortune**	*-teller, s*
for*		**forward**	*ed, ing, ly, ness, s*
forbad or **forbade**		**fossil**	*s*
forbid	*den, ding, s*	**fought*** (fight)	
force	*d, ǿing, s*	**foul*** (dirty)	*ed, ing, er, est, ly, ness, s*
ford	*ed, ing, s*	**found**	*ed, ing, er*
fore*(front)	*arm, ground, most, man, men*	**foundation**	*-stone, s*
forecast	*ing, er, s*	**foundr** *y*	*ies*
forehead	*s*	**fountain**	*-pen, s*
foreign		**fowl*** (bird)	*s* or **fowl**
foreigner	*s*	**fox**	*es, hounds, hunting, y*
forest	*ry, er, s*	**foxglove**	*s*
foretell	*ing, er, s*	**fox-terrier**	*s*
foretold		**foyer**	*s*

ǿ Drop **ė** before adding *ing*

*	for	fort	forth	foul
	fore	fought	fourth (4th)	fowl
	four (4)			

fr   fu

fr

fraction	s
fracture	d, ȩing, s
fragile	ly, ness
fragment	s
fragrance	s
fragrant	ly
frail	er, est, ly, ty, ness
frame	d, ȩing, r, work, s
franc* (foreign coin)	s
frank* (candid, etc.)	er, est, ly, ness, s
frankincense	
frantic	ally, ly
fraud	s
fray	ed, ing, s
freak	ish, s
freckle	d, ȩing, s
free	d, ing, r, st, ly, dom, -style, way, s
freeze* (ice; cold)	r, s
freezing	-point
freight	er, s
frequent	ly, ed, ing, s
fresh	er, est, ly, ness
freshen	ed, ing, er, s
fret	ted, ting, ful, fully, s
fret	work, saw, s
friar	s
Friday	s
fried	
friend	ship, s
friendly	ier, iest, iness
frieze* (wall decoration)	s
frigate	s
fright	s
frighten	ed, ing, s
frightful	ly, ness
frill	ed, ing, y, s

fringe	d, ȩing, s
frisk	ed, ing, s
frisky	ier, iest, ily, iness
fritter	ed, ing, s
frivolous	ly, ness
frizz	ed, ing, es
frizzy	ier, iest, ily, iness
frock	s
frog	-spawn, s
frolic	ked, king, some, s
front	ed, ing, s
frontier	s
frost	ed, ing, -bite, -bitten, s
frosty	ier, iest, ily, iness
froth	ed, ing, s
frothy	ier, iest, ily, iness
frown	ed, ing, s
froze	n
frugal	ity, ly
fruit	-cake, -juice, -tree, s
fry	er, ing
fried	ies

fu

fudge	
fuel	led, ling, s
fugitive	s
fulfil	led, ling, ment, s
full	er, est, y, ness
fumble	d, ȩing, r, s
fume	d, ȩing, s
fun	fair
funny	ier, iest, ily, iness
function	ed, ing, s
fund	s
funeral	s

ȩ Drop **e** before adding *ing*

* franc   freeze
  frank   frieze

ga

fungus	*es* or **fungi**			
funnel	*led, ling, s*			
fur* (animal's coat)	*rier, s*			
furr *y*	*ier, iest, ily, iness*			
furious	*ly, ness*			
furl	*ed, ing, s*			
furnace	*s*			
furnish	*ed, ing, ings, es*			
furniture				
furrow	*ed, ing, s*			
further	*ed, ing, more, most, s*			
furthest				
furtive	*ly, ness*			
fur *y*	*ies*			
furze	*s*			
fuse	*d, ȩing, s*			
fuselage	*s*			
fuss	*ed, ing, es*			
fuss *y*	*ier, iest, ily, iness*			
futile	*ly*			
future	*s*			
fuzz *y*	*ier, iest, ily, iness*			

ga

gabardine or **gaberdine**

gabble	*d, ȩing, r, s*
gag	*ged, ging, s*
gaiet *y*	*ies*
gaily	
gain	*ed, ing, s*
gait* (way of walking)	*s*
gala	*s*
galactic	
galax *y*	*ies*
gale	*s*
gallant	*ly, s*

galleon	*s*
galler *y*	*ies*
galley	*-slave, s*
gallon	*s*
gallop	*ed, ing, s*
gallows	
gamble* (bet)	*d, ȩing, r, s*
gambol* (leap; frisk)	*led, ling, s*
game	*r, st, ly, ness, keeper, s*
gander	*s*
gang	*ed, ing, ster, s*
gangway	*s*
gaol or **jail**	*ed, ing, er, s*
gape	*d, ȩing, r, s*
garage	*d, ȩing, s*
garbage	
garden	*ed, ing, er, s*
gargle	*d, ȩing, s*
garland	*ed, ing, s*
garlic	
garment	*s*
garret	*s*
garrison	*ed, ing, s*
garter	*s*
gas	*sed, sing, es*
gash	*ed, ing, es*
gasp	*ed, ing, s*
gate* (door)	*keeper, post, way, s*
gather	*ed, ing, er, s*
gaud *y*	*ier, iest, ily, iness*
gauge	*d, ȩing, s*
gauntlet	*s*
gauze	*s*
gave	
gay	*er, est*
gaily	
gaze	*d, ȩing, r, s*

ȩ Drop **e** before adding *ing*

*	fur	gait	gamble
	fir	gate	gambol

ge gh   gi gl

ge

gear	ed, ing, case, -lever, wheel, s
geese	
Geiger counter	s
gem	s
general	s
generally	
generate	d, eing, s
generation	s
generator	s
generosity	
generous	ly
genie	**genii**
genius	es
gentle	r, st, ness, man, men
gently	
genuine	ly, ness
geograph y	ical, ically
geologist	s
geolog y	ical, ically
geometr y	ic, ical, ically
Georgian	s
geranium	s
germ	s
germinate	d, eing, s
germination	s
gesticulate	d, eing, s
gesture	d, eing, s
get	ting, ter, away, s
geyser	s

gh

ghastl y	ier, iest, ily, iness
gherkin	s
ghost	s
ghostl y	ier, iest, ily, iness

gi

giant	-killer, s
gidd y	ier, iest, ily, iness
gift	ed, s
gigantic	ally
giggle	d, eing, r, s
gild* (cover with gold)	ed, ing, er, s
gilt* (gold covering)	
ginger	-ale, -beer, bread, -snap, s
gips y or **gyps** y	ies
giraffe	s
girder	s
girl	ish, -friend, s
Girl Guide	s
give	n, eing, r, s

gl

glacier	s
glad	der, dest, ly, ness
gladden	ed, ing, s
glade	s
gladiator	s
gladiolus	es or **gladioli**
glamour	
glamorous	ly
glance	d, eing, s
glare	d, eing, s
glass	es
gleam	ed, ing, s
glean	ed, ing, er, s
glee	ful, fully
glide	d, eing, r, s
glimmer	ed, ing, s
glimpse	d, eing, s
glint	ed, ing, s
glisten	ed, ing, s

e Drop **e** before adding *ing*

*	gild	gilt
	guild	guilt

gn go   gr_a

glitter	*ed, ing, s*		**golliwog**	*s*
gloat	*ed, ing, s*		**gondola**	*s*
globe	*-trotter, s*		**gondolier**	*s*
glockenspiel	*s*		**gone**	
gloom			**gong**	*s*
gloomy	*ier, iest, ily, iness*		**good**	*-hearted, ly, ness, s*
glory	*ied, ies*		**good-bye**	*s*
glorious	*ly*		**goose**	**geese**
glossy	*ier, iest, ily, iness*		**gooseberr**y	*ies*
glove	*-puppet, s*		**gore**	*d, ǵing, s*
glow	*ed, ing, -worm, s*		**gorge**	*d, ǵing, s*
glue	*d, ǵing, y, -pot, s*		**gorgeous**	*ly, ness*
glum	*mer, mest, ly, ness*		**gorilla**	*s*
			gorse	*s*
			gosling	*s*

gn

gnash	*ed, ing, es*
gnat	*-bite, s*
gnaw	*n, ed, ing, er, s*
gnome	*s*

gossip	*ed, ing, er, s*
govern	*ed, ing, or, ment, s*
governess	*es*
gown	*s*

gr

go

goal	*keeper, -kick, -mouth, -post, s*
goat	*herd, skin, s*
gobble	*d, ǵing, r, s*
goblet	*s*
goblin	*s*
god	*son, father, mother, parent, s*
goddess	*es*
godchild	*ren*
goes	
going	*s*
goggle	*d, ǵing, s*
gold	*en, -dust, -field, -mine, -smith*
goldfish	*es* or **goldfish**
golf	*ing, -club, -course, -links, er, s*

grab	*bed, bing, ber, s*
grace	*d, ǵing, s*
graceful	*ly, ness*
gracious	*ly, ness*
grade	*d, ǵing, s*
gradient	*s*
gradual	*ly, ness*
grain	*s*
grammar	
gramophone	*s*
grand	*er, est, ly, ness, stand*
grand	*father, pa, mother, ma, parents*
grandad or **grand-dad**	*s*
grandchild	*ren*
granny	*ies*

*ǵ Drop **e** before adding ing*

gre   gri   gro   gru

grange	*s*	**grill*** (cook)	*ed, ing, er, s*
granite		**grille*** (grating)	*s*
grant	*ed, ing, s*	**grim**	*mer, mest, ly, ness*
grape	*fruit, -vine, s*	**grime**	
graph	*ed, ing, s*	**grim** *y*	*ier, iest, ily, iness*
grapple	*d, ∉ing, s*	**grin**	*ned, ning, ner, s*
grasp	*ed, ing, s*	**grind**	*ing, er, stone, s*
grass	*ed, ing, es*	**grip**	*ped, ping, per, s*
grass *y*	*ier, iest, iness*	**gristle**	
grasshopper	*s*	**grit**	*ted, ting, ter, s*
grass-snake	*s*	**gritt** *y*	*ier, iest, ily, iness*
grate* (fireplace; rub)	*r,* d, ∉ing, s*	**grizzle**	*d, ∉ing, r, s*
grateful	*ly, ness*	**groan*** (moan)	*ed, ing, er, s*
grating	*s*	**grocer**	*s*
gratitude		**grocer** *y*	*ies*
grave	*r, st, ly, ness*	**groom**	*ed, ing, s*
grave	*-digger, stone, yard, s*	**groove**	*d, ∉ing, s*
gravel	*led, ling, ly, -path, -pit, s*	**grope**	*d, ∉ing, s*
gravit *y*	*ies*	**grotesque**	*ly, ness*
grav *y*	*ies*	**grotto**	*es or s*
graze	*d, ∉ing, s*	**ground**	*ed, ing, sheet, sman, smen, s*
grease	*d, ∉ing, r, -paint, -proof, s*	**group**	*ed, ing, -leader, s*
greas *y*	*ier, iest, ily, iness*	**grove**	*s*
great* (large)	*er,* est, ly, ness, s*	**grovel**	*led, ling, ler, s*
greed		**grow**	*th, ing, er, s*
greed *y*	*ier, iest, ily, iness*	**grown*** (got bigger)	
green	*er, est, ly, ness, ery, ish, y, s*	**grown-up**	*s*
greengrocer	*s*	**growl**	*ed, ing, er, s*
greenhouse	*s*	**grub**	*bed, bing, ber, s*
greet	*ed, ing, s*	**grubb** *y*	*ier, iest, ily, iness*
grenade	*s*	**grudge**	*d, ∉ing, s*
grenadier	*s*	**gruel**	
grew		**gruesome**	*ly, ness*
grey	*er, est, ly, ness, ish, hound, s*	**gruff**	*er, est, ly, ness*
grief	*-stricken, s*	**grumble**	*d, ∉ing, r, s*
grievance	*s*	**grump** *y*	*ier, iest, ily, iness*
grieve	*d, ∉ing, s*	**grunt**	*ed, ing, er, s*

*∉ Drop **e** before adding* ing

*	grate	grater	grill	groan
	great	greater	grille	grown

gu gy ha

gu

guarantee	*d, ing, s*
guard	*ed, ing, sman, smen, room, s*
guardian	*s*
guess	*ed,* ing, es, work*
guest* (visitor)	*-night, -house, -room, s*
guide	*d, ǿing, -dog, -book, -post, s*
guild* (society)	*hall, s*
guillotine	*d, ǿing, s*
guilt* (wrongdoing)	*less, lessly*
guilt *y*	*ier, iest, ily, iness*
guinea-pig	*s*
guitar	*ist, s*
gulf	*s*
gull	*s*
gull *y*	*ies*
gulp	*ed, ing, s*
gum	*med, ming, boil, -tree, s*
gumm *y*	*ier, iest, iness*
gun	*ned, ning, ner, nery, man, men, s*
gun	*fire, point, powder, shot, smith, s*
gurgle	*d, ǿing, s*
gush	*ed, ing, es*
gust	*ed, ing, s*
gust *y*	*ier, iest, ily, iness*
gut	*ted, ting, s*
gutter	*s*
guy	*s*
guzzle	*d, ǿing, r, s*

gy

gymkhana	*s*
gymnasium	*s* or **gymnasia**
gymnast	*ic, s*
gymslip	*s*
gyps *y* or **gips** *y*	*ies*

ha

habit	*s*
hack	*ed, ing, er, s*
haddock	*s* or **haddock**
hadn't (had not)	
hail	*ed, ing, er, stone, storm, s*
hair*	*dresser, -dryer, pin, -slide, -style, s*
hair *y*	*ier, iest, iness*
hake	*s* or **hake**
half	*-price, -term, -time, -way,* **halves**
halfpenn *y*	*ies* or **halfpence**
hall* (room; passage)	*way, s*
hallo or **hello** or **hullo**	*ed, ing, s*
halo	*es* or *s*
halt	*ed, ing, s*
halve	*d, ǿing, s*
hamburger	*s*
hammer	*ed, ing, s*
hammock	*s*
hamper	*ed, ing, s*
hamster	*s*
hand	*ed, ing, bag, work, writing, ful, s*
handcuff	*ed, ing, s*
handicap	*ped, ping, per, s*
handicraft	
handiwork	
handkerchief	*s*
handle	*d, ǿing, r, -bar, s*
handsome	*r, st, ly, ness*
hand *y*	*ier, iest, ily, iness*
hang	*ed, ing, -gliding, -glider, s*
hangar* (aeroplane shed)	*s*
hanger* (for clothes, etc.)	*s*
happen	*ed, ing, s*
happ *y*	*ier, iest, ily, iness*
harbour	*ed, ing, -master, s*
hard	*er, est, ish, ly, ness, -hearted, ware*

*ǿ Drop **e** before adding ing*

*	guessed	guild	guilt		hair	hall	hangar
	guest	gild	gilt		hare	haul	hanger

he

harden	ed, ing, er, s
hardship	s
hare* (animal)	s
hark	en
harm	ed, ing, s
harmful	ly, ness
harmless	ly, ness
harness	ed, ing, es
harp	ist, s
harpoon	ed, ing, -gun, s
harsh	er, est, ly, ness
hart* (stag)	s
harvest	ed, ing, er, s
hasn't (has not)	
haste	d, ∉ing, s
hasten	ed, ing, s
hast y	ier, iest, ily, iness
hat	band, -peg, -pin, stand, -trick, ful, s
hatch	ed, ing, es
hatchet	s
hate	d, ∉ing, r, s
hateful	ly, ness
hatred	
haught y	ier, iest, ily, iness
haul* (pull)	age, ed, ing, ier, s
haunt	ed, ing, s
have	∉ing
haven't (have not)	
haversack	s
havoc	
haw	thorn, s
hawk	ed, ing, er, s
hay	field, maker, making, rick, stack, s
hazard	ed, ing, ous, ously, s
hazel	nut, -tree, s
haze	s
haz y	ier, iest, ily, iness

he

head	ed, ing, ache, long, light, way, s
headmaster	s
headmistress	es
headquarters	
heal* (cure)	ed, ing, er, s
health	
health y	ier, iest, ily, iness
heap	ed, ing, s
hear* (listen)	ing, s
heard* (listened)	
heart* (of body)	ache, -broken, less, s
hearten	ed, ing, s
heart y	ier, iest, ily, iness
hearth	-rug, s
heat	ed, edly, ing, er, -stroke, wave, s
heath	land, s
heathen	s
heather	s
heave	d, ∉ing, r, s
heaven	ly, ward, s
heav y	ier, iest, ily, iness
he'd (he had; he would)	
hedge	d, ∉ing, hog, row, -sparrow, s
heed	ed, ing, ful, less, s
heel* (back of foot)	ed, ing, s
heft y	ier, iest, ily, iness
heifer	s
height	s
heighten	ed, ing, s
heir* (one who inherits)	loom, s
heiress	es
held	
helicopter	s
he'll (he will; he shall)	
hello or **hallo** or **hullo**	ed, ing, s
helm	sman, smen, s

∉ Drop **e** before adding *ing*

*	hare	haul	hart	heal	hear	he'ard	heir
	hair	hall	heart	heel	here	herd	air

hi   ho

helmet	*s*
help	*ed, ing, er, s*
helpful	*ly, ness*
helpless	*ly, ness*
helter-skelter	*s*
hem	*med, ming, -line, s*
her	*self, s*
herald	*ed, ing, s*
herb	*age, al, alist, s*
herd* (of cattle, etc.)	*ed, ing, sman, s*
here* (in this place)	*about(s), by, with*
here's (here is)	
hermit	*age, -crab, s*
hero	*es*
heroic	*al, ally, s*
heroine	*s*
heroism	
heron	*s*
herring	*-gull, s* or **herring**
he's (he is; he has)	
hesitate	*d, ∉ing, s*
hesitation	*s*
hew* (chop; cut)	*n, ed, ing, er, s*
hexagon	*al, s*

hi

hibernate	*d, ∉ing, s*
hibernation	
hiccup	*ed, ing, s*
hid	*den*
hide	*∉ing, -and-seek, away, -out, s*
hideous	*ly, ness*
high	*er*, est, ly, chair, light, -road, s*
highland	*er, s*
Highness	*es*
highway	*man, men, s*

hijack	*ed, ing, er, s*
hike	*d, ∉ing, r, s*
hilarious	*ly, ness*
hill	*ock, side, top, s*
hill *y*	*ier, iest, iness*
him* (he)	*self*
hinder	*ed, ing, s*
hindrance	*s*
hinge	*d, ∉ing, s*
hint	*ed, ing, s*
hippopotamus	*es* or **hippopotami**
hire* (rent)	*d, ∉ing, -purchase, r, s*
hiss	*ed, ing, es*
historic	*al, ally*
histor *y*	*ies*
hit	*ting, ter, s*
hitch	*ed, ing, es*
hitch-hike	*d, ∉ing, r, s*
hive	*s*

ho

hoard* (hidden store)	*ed, ing, s*
hoarse* (husky)	*r, st, ly, ness*
hobble	*d, ∉ing, s*
hobb *y*	*ies*
hockey	*-stick*
hoe	*d, ing, s*
hog	*skin, s*
hoist	*ed, ing, s*
hold	*ing, -all, -up, er, s*
hole* (hollow place)	*d, ∉ing, s*
holiday	*ed, ing, -camp, -maker, s*
hollow	*ed, ing, ly, ness, s*
holl *y*	*ies*
hollyhock	*s*
holster	*s*

*∉ Drop **e** before adding ing*

herd	here	hew	higher	him	hoard	hoarse	hole
heard	hear	hue	hire	hymn	horde	horse	whole

hol y* (godly)	*ier, iest, ily, iness, ies*
home	*-grown, -made, work, ward, s*
homeless	*ness*
homel y	*ier, iest, iness*
homesick	*ness*
honest	*ly, y*
honey	*-bee, dew, -pot, comb, suckle, s*
honeymoon	*ed, ing, er, s*
honour	*able, ably, ed, ing, s*
hood	*ed, ing, s*
hoof	*beat, mark, s* or **hooves**
hook	*ed, ing, er, s*
hooligan	*ism, s*
hoop	*ed, ing, -la, s*
hoot	*ed, ing, er, s*
hop	*ped, ping, per, s*
hope	*d, ∉ing, s*
hopeful	*ly, ness*
hopeless	*ly, ness*
horde* (crowd)	*s*
horizon	*tal, tally, s*
horn	*s*
hornpipe	*s*
hornet	*s*
horoscope	*s*
horrible	*ness*
horribly	
horrid	*ly, ness*
horrify	*ing*
horrif ied	*ies*
horror	*-stricken, -struck, s*
horse* (animal)	*back, man, men, shoe, s*
horse-chestnut	*-tree, s*
hose	*d, ∉ing, -pipe, s*
hospital	*s*
hospitality	
host	*s*

hostage	*s*
hostel	*led, ling, ler, s*
hostess	*es*
hostile	*ly*
hot	*ter, test, ly, ness, house, -plate*
hotel	*ier, s*
hound	*ed, ing, s*
hour* (sixty mins.)	*ly, -hand, s*
house	*d, ∉ing, hold, work, keeper, s*
housemaster	*s*
housemistress	*es*
house wife	*wives*
hover	*ed, ing, port, s, craft*
however	
howl	*ed, ing, er, s*

hu

huddle	*d, ∉ing, s*
hue* (colour)	*s*
hug	*ged, ging, s*
huge	*r, st, ly, ness*
hullo or **hallo** or **hello**	*ed, ing, s*
hum	*med, ming, mer, s*
human	*ity, ly*
humble	*d, ∉ing, r, st, ness, s*
humbly	
humid	*ity*
humiliate	*d, ∉ing, s*
humorous	*ly, ness*
humour	*ed, ing, s*
hump	*ed, ing, s*
hunch	*ed, ing, s*
hundred	*th, weight, s*
hung	
hunger	*ed, ing, s*
hungr y	*ier, iest, ily, iness*

*∉ Drop **e** before adding* ing

*	holy	horde	horse		hour	hue
	wholly	hoard	hoarse		our	hew

hy   ic   id   ig   il

hunt	ed, ing, sman, smen, er, s
hurdle	d, ǿing, r, s
hurl	ed, ing, er, s
hurrah or **hurray**	ed, ing, s
hurricane	-lamp, s
hurry	ing
hurr ied	iedly, ies
hurt	ing, s
hurtle	d, ǿing, s
husband	s
hush	ed, ing, es
husk y	ier, iest, ily, iness
hustle	d, ǿing, s
hutch	es

hy

hyacinth	s
hydrangea	s
hydraulic	ally, s
hydrofoil	s
hydrogen	
hydroplane	s
hyena or **hyaena**	s
hygiene	
hygienic	ally
hymn* (song of praise)	al, -book, s
hypnotism	
hypnotist	s
hypnotize	d, ǿing, s
hysteric	al, ally, s

ic

ice	d, ǿing, berg, -cream, -cube, s
icicle	s
ic y	ier, iest, ily, iness

id

I'd (I would; I should; I had)	
idea	s
ideal	ly, ism, ist, s
identical	ly
identification	
identify	ing
identif ied	ies
identit y	ies
idiot	s
idiotic	al, ally
idle* (lazy)	d, ǿing, r, st, ness, s
idly	
idol* (false god)	s
idolize	d, ǿing, s

ig

igloo	s
ignite	d, ǿing, s
ignorance	
ignorant	ly
ignore	d, ǿing, s

il

I'll (I will)	
ill	-bred, -mannered, -treated, s
illness	es
illegal	ly
illegible	
illiterate	ly, ness, s
illuminate	d, ǿing, s
illumination	s
illusion	ist, s
illustrate	d, ǿing, s
illustration	s

ǿ Drop **e** before adding *ing*

*	hymn	idle
	him	idol

im

in

im

I'm (I am)	
image	*s*
imaginary	
imagination	*s*
imagine	*d, ǿing, s*
imitate	*d, ǿing, s*
imitation	*s*
immediate	*ly, ness*
immense	*ly, ness*
immortal	*ity, ly, s*
immune	
immunize	*d, ǿing, s*
impatience	
impatient	*ly*
imperfect	*ion, ly*
impersonate	*d, ǿing, s*
impersonation	*s*
impertinence	*s*
impertinent	*ly*
implement	*s*
implore	*d, ǿing, s*
impolite	*ly, ness*
impórt	*ed, ing, er, s*
importance	
important	*ly*
impose	*d, ǿing, s*
impossibility	*ies*
impossible	
impress	*ed, ing, ive, es*
impression	*able, s*
imprison	*ed, ing, ment, s*
improve	*d, ǿing, ment, s*
impudence	
impudent	*ly*
impure	*ly*
impurity	*ies*

in

inaccurate	*ly*
inattentive	*ly, ness*
incapable	
inch	*ed, ing, es*
incident	*al, ally, s*
incline	*d, ǿing, s*
include	*d, ǿing, s*
inclusive	*ly, ness*
income	*s*
inconvenience	*d, ǿing, s*
inconvenient	*ly*
incorrect	*ly, ness*
increase	*d, ǿing, s*
incredible	*y*
incurable	*ness, s*
indeed	
indefinite	*ly, ness*
independent	*ly*
indicate	*d, ǿing, s*
indication	*s*
indicator	*s*
indigestion	
indignant	*ly*
indignation	
indistinct	*ly, ness*
individual	*ly, s*
indoor	*s*
industrial	*ly*
industrious	*ly*
industry	*ies*
inexpensive	*ly, ness*
infant	*s*
infantry	*man, men*
infect	*ed, ing, ious, ion, s*
inferior	*ity, ly, s*
infirmary	*ies*

ǿ Drop **e** before adding *ing*

inflammable	*ness*
inflate	*d, ∅ing, s*
influence	*d, ∅ing, s*
influenza	
inform	*ed, ing, ation, er, s*
infrequent	*ly*
infuriate	*d, ∅ing, s*
ingredient	*s*
inhabit	*ed, ing, able, ant, s*
inhale	*d, ∅ing, s*
inherit	*ed, ing, ance, s*
initial	*led, ling, s*
inject	*ed, ing, ion, s*
injure	*d, ∅ing, s*
injur *y*	*ies*
ink	*ed, ing, -bottle, -pot, stand, -well, s*
ink *y*	*ier, iest, iness*
inland	
inn	*keeper, s*
inner	*most*
innings	
innocence	
innocent	*ly, s*
inoculate	*d, ∅ing, s*
inoculation	*s*
inquire or **enquire**	*d, ∅ing, r, s*
inquir *y* or **enquir** *y*	*ies*
inquisitive	*ly, ness*
insane	*ly*
inscription	*s*
insect	*s*
insensible	
insert	*ed, ing, ion, s*
inside	*s*
insist	*ed, ing, ence, ent, s*
insolence	
insolent	*ly*

inspect	*ed, ing, ion, or, s*
inspiration	*s*
inspire	*d, ∅ing, s*
install	*ed, ing, ation, s*
instalment	*s*
instance	*s*
instant	*aneous, ly*
instead	
instinct	*ive, ively, s*
institute	*d, ∅ing, s*
institution	*al, s*
instruct	*ed, ing, ive, ion, or, s*
instrument	*al, alist, s*
insufficient	*ly*
insult	*ed, ing, s*
insurance	*s*
insure	*d, ∅ing, s*
intact	
intelligence	
intelligent	*ly*
intend	*ed, ing, s*
intense	*ly, ness*
intent	*ly, ness*
intention	*al, ally, s*
intercept	*ed, ing, ive, ion, or s*
interest	*ed, ing, s*
interfere	*d, ∅ing, nce, s*
interior	*s*
interlude	*s*
intermediate	*ly*
international	*ly*
interpret	*ed, ing, ation, er, s*
interrogate	*d, ∅ing, s*
interrupt	*ed, ing, ion, s*
interval	*s*
intervene	*d, ∅ing, s*
interview	*ed, ing, er, s*

*∅ Drop **e** before adding *ing*

introduce	d, ∉ing, s
introduction	s
intrude	d, ∉ing, r, s
invade	d, ∉ing, r, s
invalid	ed, ing, s
invasion	s
invent	ed, ing, ive, ion, or, s
investigate	d, ∉ing, s
investigation	s
investigator	s
invisible	ness
invitation	s
invite	d, ∉ing, s
involve	d, ∉ing, s
inward	ly, s

ir

iris	es
iron	ed, ing, monger, work, s
ironing-board	s
irregular	ity, ly
irrigate	d, ∉ing, s
irrigation	
irritable	y
irritability	ies
irritate	d, ∉ing, s
irritation	s

is

island	er, s
isle* (island)	s
isn't (is not)	
isolate	d, ∉ing, s
isolation	
issue	d, ∉ing, s

it

italic	s
itch	ed, ing, es
itchy	ier, iest, iness
item	s
its* (belonging to it)	
it's* (it is)	
itself	

iv

I've (I have)	
ivory	ies
ivy	ies

ja

jab	bed, bing, s
jabber	ed, ing, s
jack	ed, ing, pot, s
jackdaw	s
jacket	s
jade	d, ∉ing, s
jagged	ly, ness
jaguar	s
jail or **gaol**	ed, ing, er, s
jam	med, ming, my, -pot, -jar, s
jamboree	s
jangle	d, ∉ing, s
January	s
jar	red, ring, ful, s
jaunt	ed, ing, s
jaunty	ier, iest, ily, iness
javelin	s
jaw	-bone, s
jay	s
jazz	ed, ing, y, es

∉ Drop **e** before adding *ing*

* isle	its
aisle	it's

je ji jo   ju

je

jealous	*ly*
jealous *y*	*ies*
jeans	
jeep	*s*
jeer	*ed, ing, s*
jell *y*	*ied, ies*
jelly-fish	*es* or **jelly-fish**
jemm *y*	*ies*
jerk	*ed, ing, s*
jerk *y*	*ier, iest, ily, iness*
jerkin	*s*
jersey	*s*
jest	*ed, ing, er, s*
jet	*ted, ting, -liner, -plane, -fighter, s*
jettison	*ed, ing, s*
jett *y*	*ies*
Jew*	*ish, s*
jewel*	*led, ling, ler, -case, s*
jewellery or **jewelry**	

ji

jiff *y*	*ies*
jig	*ged, ging, ger, s*
jigsaw puzzle	*s*
jilt	*ed, ing, s*
jingle	*d, ǿing, -jangle, s*
jiu-jitsu or **ju-jitsu** or **judo**	
jive	*d, ǿing, s*

jo

job	*less, s*
jockey	*s*
jocular	*ity, ly*
jodhpurs	

ju (right column top)

jog	*ged, ging, ger, s*
join	*ed, ing, ery, er, s*
joint	*ed, ing, ly, s*
joist	*s*
joke	*d, ǿing, r, s*
jollit *y*	*ies*
joll *y*	*ier, iest, ily, iness*
jolt	*ed, ing, s*
jonquil	*s*
jostle	*d, ǿing, s*
jot	*ted, ting, ter, s*
journal	*ism, ist, s*
journey	*ed, ing, s*
joust	*ed, ing, s*
jovial	*ity, ly*
joy	*s*
joyful	*ly, ness*
joyous	*ly, ness*

ju

jubilant	*ly*
jubilation	*s*
jubilee	*s*
judge	*d, ǿing, s*
judg(e)ment	*s*
judo or **ju-jitsu** or **jiu-jitsu**	
juggle	*d, ǿing, r, s*
juice	*s*
juic *y*	*ier, iest, ily, iness*
July	*s*
jumble	*d, ǿing, -sale, s*
jump	*ed, ing, er, -jet, s*
jumper	*s*
jump *y*	*ier, iest, ily, iness*
junction	*s*
June	*s*

ǿ Drop **e** before adding *ing*

*	Jew	jewel
	dew	dual
	due	duel

jungle	s
junior	s
junk	-shop, s
junket	s
juror	s
jur y	ies
just	ly, ness
justice	
justify	ing
justif ied	ies
jut	ted, ting, s
juvenile	s

ka

kaleidoscope	s
kangaroo	s
karate	
kayak	s

ke

keel	ed, ing, s
keen	er, est, ly, ness
keep	ing, er, sake, s
kennel	-maid, s
kept	
kerb* (pavement edge)	side, stone, s
kernel* (nut; seed)	s
kestrel	s
ketchup	
kettle	-holder, ful, s
key*	hole, -ring, s

kh

khaki	s

ki

kick	ed, ing, -off, er, s
kid	skin, s
kidnap	ped, ping, per, s
kidney	-bean, s
kill	ed, ing, er, s
kiln	s
kilogram(me)	s
kilometre	s
kilt	s
kimono	s
kin	sfolk, sman, smen
kind	er, est, -hearted, s
kindl y	ier, iest, ily, iness
kindness	es
kindergarten	s
kindle	d, ɇing, s
king	dom, cup, fisher, s
kink	ed, ing, y, s
kiosk	s
kipper	s
kiss	ed, ing, es
kit	ted, ting, -bag, s
kitchen	ette, -maid, s
kite	s
kitten	s

kn

knack	s
knapsack	s
knave* (rogue)	s
knead* (work dough)	ed, ing, s
knee	-deep, -high, -cap, s
kneel	ed, ing, s
knelt or kneeled	
knew* (know)	

ɇ Drop e before adding ing

*	kerb	kernel	key	knave	knead	knew
	curb	colonel	quay	nave	need	new

la

knife	*d, ∅ing, -edge, -point,* **knives**
knight* (Sir)	*ed, ing, ly, -errant, hood, s*
knit	*ted, ting, ter, s*
knitting-needle	*s*
knob	*s*
knobbl *y*	*ier, iest, iness*
knock	*ed, ing, er, -out, s*
knot* (tied string; sea speed)	*ted, ting, s*
knott *y*	*ier, iest, ily, iness*
know* (understand)	*n, ing, ingly, s*
knowledge	*able*
knuckle	*d, ∅ing, -bone, -duster, s*

la

label	*led, ling, s*
laborator *y*	*ies*
labour	*ed, ing, er, s*
lace	*d, ∅ing, s*
lack	*ed, ing, s*
lacquer	*ed, ing, s*
lacrosse	
ladder	*ed, ing, s*
laden	
lad *y*	*ies*
ladybird	*s*
lag	*ged, ging, gard, s*
lagoon	*s*
laid	
lain* (lie flat)	
lair* (den)	*s*
lake	*s*
lamb	*ed, ing, -chop, kin, skin, swool, s*
lame	*d, ∅ing, r, st, ly, ness, s*
lament	*ed, ing, able, ation, s*
lamp	*light, -post, shade, -standard, s*
lance	*d, ∅ing, -corporal, r, s*

land	*ed, ing, mark, scape, slide, slip, s*
landlad *y*	*ies*
landlord	*s*
lane* (narrow road)	*s*
language	*s*
lantern	*s*
lap	*ped, ping, s*
lapel	*s*
lapse	*d, ∅ing, s*
larch	*es*
lard	*ed, ing, s*
larder	*s*
large	*r, st, ly, ness*
lark	*s*
larva* (insect grub)	*e*
lash	*ed, ing, es*
lass	*es*
lasso	*ed, ing, es* or *s*
last	*ed, ing, ly, s*
latch	*ed, ing, es*
late	*r, st, ly, ness*
lathe	*s*
lather	*ed, ing, s*
latitude	*s*
latter	*ly*
laugh	*able, ed, ing, s*
laughter	
launch	*ed, ing, es*
launder	*ette, ed, ing, s*
laundress	*es*
laundr *y*	*ies*
laurel	*s*
lava* (volcanic rock)	*s*
lavator *y*	*ies*
lavender	*-water*
law	*ful, less, -breaker, -court, s*
lawyer	*s*

∅ Drop **e** before adding *ing*

*	knight	knot	know		lain	lair	larva
	night	not	no		lane	layer	lava

le

lawn   -mower, -sprinkler, s
lay   ing, about, -by, out, er, s
laid
layer* (coat; thickness)   ed, ing, s
laze   d, ǿing, s
laz y   ier, iest, ily, iness

le

lead* (metal)   ed, en, -poisoning, s
lead (be first)   ing, er, s
leaf   ed, ing, less, -stalk, **leaves**
leaf y   ier, iest, iness
leaflet   s
league   s
leak* (hole; crack)   age, ed, ing, s
leak y   ier, iest, iness
lean   er, est, ly, ness
lean   ed, ing, s
leant* or **leaned**
leap   ed, ing, frog, -year, s
leapt or **leaped**
learn   ed, ing, er, s
learnt or **learned**
least
leather   y, s
leave   ǿing, r, s
lecture   d, ǿing, r, s
led* (guided)
ledge   s
leek* (vegetable)   s
left
leg   ged, ging, less, -iron, -rest, s
legend   ary, s
legion   s
leisure   ly
lemon   ade, -drop, -juice, -peel, -tree, s

li

lend   ing, er, s
length   s
lengthen   ed, ing, s
length y   ier, iest, ily, iness
lenient   ly
lens   es
lent* (lend)
leopard   skin, s
leotard   s
leper   s
leprosy
less   er
lessen* (make smaller)   ed, ing, s
lesson* (thing learnt)   s
let   ting, s
let's (let us)
letter   ed, ing, -writer, s
letter-box   es
lettuce   s
level   led, ling, -crossing, s
lever   age, ed, ing, s

li

liable
liar* (one who lies)   s
liberal   s
libert y   ies
librarian   s
librar y   ies
licence* (noun)   s
license* (verb)   d, ǿing, s
lick   ed, ing, er, s
licorice or **liquorice**
lie   d, s
lying
lieutenant -colonel, -general, s

ǿ Drop **e** before adding ing

lo

life	*less, like, line, long, size, time.* **lives**
life	*boat, belt, -guard, -jacket, -saving*
lift	*ed, ing, er, s*
light	*er, est, ly, ness, weight, s*
light	*ed, ing, ish, er, house, ship, s*
lighten	*ed, ing, s*
lightning	*-conductor*
like	*able, d, ǿing, ness, s*
likely	*ier, iest, ihood*
lilac	*-tree, s*
lily	*ies*
limb	*less, s*
lime	*-juice, light, -tree, s*
limit	*ed, ing, less, s*
limp	*ed, ing, er, est, ly, ness, s*
limpet	*s*
line	*d, ǿing, sman, smen, s*
linen	*s*
liner	*s*
linger	*ed, ing, er, s*
link	*ed, ing, s*
linoleum or **lino**	*s*
lion	*-tamer, s*
lioness	*es*
lip	*-reading, stick, s*
liquid	*s*
liquorice or **licorice**	
list	*ed, ing, s*
listen	*ed, ing, er, s*
lit or **lighted**	
literature	
litter	*ed, ing, -basket, -bin, -bug, -lout, s*
little	*ness*
live	*d, ǿing, r, s*
lively	*ier, iest, ily, iness*
liver	*ish, s*
lizard	*s*

lo

load	*ed, ing, er, s*
loaf	**loaves**
loan* (lend)	*ed, ing, s*
loathe	*d, ǿing, s*
loathsome	*ly, ness*
lob	*bed, bing, ber, s*
lobby	*ies*
lobster	*-pot, s*
local	*ly, s*
locality	*ies*
locate	*d, ǿing, s*
location	*s*
lock	*ed, ing, er, smith, s*
locket	*s*
locomotive	*s*
locust	*s*
lodge	*d, ǿing, r, s*
loft	*s*
lofty	*ier, iest, ily, iness*
log	*ged, ging, -book, -cabin, s*
loganberry	*ies*
loiter	*ed, ing, er, s*
loll	*ed, ing, er, s*
lollipop	*s*
lolly	*ies*
lone* (alone)	*r, some*
lonely	*ier, iest, ily, iness*
long	*ed, ing, ingly, er, est, bow, -stop, s*
longitude	*s*
look	*ed, ing, er, -out, s*
looking-glass	*es*
loom	*ed, ing, s*
loop	*ed, ing, hole, s*
loose	*r, st, ly, ness*
loosen	*ed, ing, s*
loot* (plunder)	*ed, ing, er, s*

*ǿ Drop **e** before adding ing*

*	loan	loot
	lone	lute

lu   ly ma

lop	ped, ping, -sided, s
lord	ship, s
lorr y	ies
lose	ẹing, r, s
loss	es
lost	
lotion	s
lotto	
loud	er, est, ish, ly, ness, -speaker
lounge	d, ẹing, r, s
lout	ish, s
love	d, ẹing, r, bird, -letter, -song, s
lovel y	ier, iest, ily, iness
low	er, est, ly, ness, s
lower	ed, ing, s
lowland	er, s
loyal	ist, ly, ty
lozenge	s

lu

lubricate	d, ẹing, s
lubrication	
luck	less
luck y	ier, iest, ily, iness
ludo	
lug	ged, ging, s
luggage	-carrier, -rack, -van
lukewarm	ly, ness
lull	ed, ing, s
lullab y	ies
lumbago	s
lumber	ed, ing, er, jack, -room, s
luminous	ly, ness
lump	ed, ing, s
lump y	ier, iest, ily, iness
lunatic	s

lunch	ed, ing, -box, es
luncheon	s
lung	s
lunge	d, ẹing, s
lupin	s
lurch	ed, ing, es
lure	d, ẹing, s
lurk	ed, ing, er, s
luscious	ly, ness
lustr e	ous
lust y	ier, iest, ily, iness
lute* (musical instrument)	s
luxuriant	ly
luxurious	ly, ness
luxur y	ies

ly

lying	
lynch	ed, ing, es
lynx	es or **lynx**
lyre* (musical instrument)	s
lyric	al, s

ma

macaroni	
mace	-bearer, s
machine	d, ẹing, -gun, s
machinery	
machinist	s
mackerel	s or **mackerel**
mackintosh	es
mad	der, dest, ly, ness, house, man, men
madden	ed, ing, s
madam	s
madame (French)	**mesdames**

ẹ Drop **e** before adding *ing*

*	lute	lyre
	loot	liar

made* (make)		**maniac**	*s*	
magazine	*s*	**manicure**	*d, ∅ing, s*	
maggot	*y, s*	**manner*** (way; behaviour)	*ed, s*	
magic	*al, ally*	**manoeuvre**	*d, ∅ing, s*	
magician	*s*	**manor*** (lord's land)	*-house, s*	
magistrate	*s*	**mansion**	*s*	
magnet	*ic, ically, ism, s*	**mantelpiece**	*s*	
magnetize	*d, ∅ing, s*	**manual**	*ly, s*	
magnificent	*ly*	**manufacture**	*d, ∅ing, r, s*	
magnify	*ing*	**manure**	*d, ∅ing, s*	
magnified	*ies*	**manuscript**	*s*	
magpie	*s*	**many**		
maid* (girl)	*en, servant, s*	**map** *ped, ping, per, -reading, s*		
mail* (armour; post)	*ed, ing, -bag, s*	**marble**	*s*	
maim	*ed, ing, s*	**March**	*es*	
main* (chief)	*ly, land, stay, s*	**march**	*ed, ing, es*	
maintain	*ed, ing, s*	**mare*** (female horse)	*s*	
maison(n)ette	*s*	**margarine**	*s*	
maize* (corn)		**margin**	*s*	
majesty	*ic, ically, ies*	**marigold**	*s*	
major	*ette, -general, s*	**marine**	*r, s*	
majority	*ies*	**marionette**	*s*	
make *∅ing, -believe, shift, -up, r, s*		**mark** *ed, ing, sman, smen, er, s*		
malaria		**market** *ed, ing, -day, -place, -stall, s*		
male* (man; masculine)	*s*	**marmalade**	*s*	
mallet	*s*	**maroon**	*ed, ing, s*	
mammal	*s*	**marquee**	*s*	
mammoth	*s*	**marriage**	*s*	
man *ned, ning, hole, hood,* **men**		**marry**	*ing*	
manly	*ier, iest, ily, iness*	**marr**ied	*ies*	
manage *d, ∅ing, able, ably, ment, s*		**marrow**	*s*	
manager	*s*	**Mars**		
manageress	*es*	**marsh**	*es*	
mandolin	*s*	**marsh**y	*ier, iest, iness*	
mane* (hair)	*s*	**marshal**	*led, ling, s*	
manger	*s*	**marsh-mallow**	*s*	
mangle	*d, ∅ing, s*	**martyr**	*ed, ing, dom, s*	

∅ Drop **e** before adding *ing*

*	made	mail	main	maize	manner	mare
	maid	male	mane	maze	manor	mayor

marvel led, ling, s
marvellous ly, ness
marzipan
mascot s
masculine s
mash ed, ing, es
mask ed, ing, s
mason ry, s
masquerade d, ∉ing, r, s
mass ed, ing, es
massacre d, ∉ing, s
massage d, ∉ing, s
masseur s
masseuse s
massive ly, ness
mast ed, -head, s
master ed, ing, ly, y, mind, piece, s
mat ted, ting, s
matador s
match ed, ing, sticks, wood, box, es
mate d, ∉ing, s
material s
mathematic al, ally, ian, s
matinée s
matron s
matter ed, ing, s
mattress es
maul ed, ing, s
mauve r, st, s
maximum a
may be
May s
maypole s
mayonnaise
mayor* (head of town or city) s
mayoress es
maze* (puzzle) s

me

meadow s
meagre ly, ness
meal -time, s
mean er, est, ly, ness, s
meaning less, s
meant
meantime
meanwhile
measles
measure d, ∉ing, ment, s
meat* (flesh) y, -axe, -ball, -pie, s
mechanic al, ally, s
mechanism s
mechanize d, ∉ing, s
medal* (badge—for bravery, etc.) s
medallion s
meddle* (interfere) d, ∉ing, some, r, s
medi(a)eval
medical ly, s
medicine s
Mediterranean
medium s or **media**
meek er, est, ly, ness
meet* (come together) ing, s
megaphone s
melody ious, iously, ies
melon s
melt ed, ing, s
member ship, s
memorial s
memorize d, ∉ing, s
memory ies
menace d, ∉ing, s
menagerie s
mend ed, ing, er, s
mental ity, ly

∉ Drop **e** before adding *ing*

* maze mayor meat medal
maize mare meet meddle

mi

mention	*ed, ing, s*		**might**	
menu	*s*		**might** *y*	*ier, iest, ily, iness*
merchant	*s*		**migrate**	*d, ⌀ing, s*
merciful	*ly, ness*		**migration**	*s*
merciless	*ly, ness*		**mild**	*er, est, ly, ness*
merc *y*	*ies*		**mildew**	*ed, ⌀ing, s*
mercury			**mile**	*age, stone, s*
mere	*ly*		**military**	
meringue	*s*		**milk**	*ed, ing, er, man, men, -shake, s*
merit	*ed, ing, s*		**milk** *y*	*ier, iest, ily, iness*
mermaid	*s*		**mill**	*ed, ing, er, -pond, stone, s*
merr *y*	*ier, iest, ily, iment*		**millimetre**	*s*
mesmerize	*d, ⌀ing, s*		**million**	*th, s*
mess	*ed, ing, es*		**millionaire**	*s*
mess *y*	*ier, iest, ily, iness*		**millionairess**	*es*
message	*s*		**mime**	*d, ⌀ing, s*
messenger	*s*		**mimic**	*ked, king, s*
metal	*lic, work, -detector, s*		**mince**	*d, ⌀ing, r, meat, -pie, s*
meteor	*ic, ite, oid, ology, ologist, s*		**mind***	*ed, ing, er, ful, less, -reader, s*
meter* (measuring box)	*s*		**mine**	*d,* * *⌀ing, field, sweeper, s*
method	*ical, ically, s*		**miner*** (mine worker)	*s*
methylated spirit(s)			**mineral**	*s*
metre* (length measure)	*s*		**mingle**	*d, ⌀ing, s*
mew	*ed, ing, s*		**miniature**	*s*
			minim *um*	*a*

mi

			minister	*s*
miaow	*ed, ing, s*		**minnow**	*s*
mice			**minor*** (young person; lesser)	*s*
microphone	*s*		**minstrel**	*s*
microscope	*s*		**mint**	*ed, ing, y, -sauce, s*
midday			**minus**	*es*
middle	*-aged, -class*		**minute**	*-hand, s*
midge	*s*		**minute** (small)	*ly, ness*
midget	*s*		**miracle**	*s*
midnight			**miraculous**	*ly, ness*
midst			**mirage**	*s*
midway			**mirror**	*ed, ing, s*

⌀ Drop **e** before adding *ing*

*	meter		mind	miner
	metre		mined	minor

mo

mirth	
misbehave	d, ℮ing, s
misbehaviour	
mischief	-maker
mischievous	ly, ness
miser	ly, s
miserabl e	y
miser y	ies
misfortune	s
mishap	s
mislay	ing, s
mislaid	
misplace	d, ℮ing, s
miss	ed*, ing, es
missile	s
mission	s
missionar y	ies
mist* (haze; fog)	ed, ing, s
mist y	ier, iest, ily, iness
mistake	n, ℮ing, s
mistook	
mistletoe	
mistress	es
mistrust	ed, ing, s
mitten	s
mix	ed, ing, es
mixer	s
mixture	s

mo

moan* (groan)	ed, ing, er, s
moat	ed, s
mob	bed, bing, s
mobile	s
moccasin	s
mock	ed, ing, s

mocker y	ies
model	led, ling, ler, s
moderate	d, ℮ing, ly, ness, s
modern	ity, ly, ness, s
modernize	d, ℮ing, s
modest	ly, y
moist	ure, ly, ness
moisten	ed, ing, s
mole	hill, skin, s
moment	s
monarch	s
monaster y	ies
Monday	s
money	-lender, -order, -spider, s
mongrel	s
monitor	s
monitress	es
monk	s
monkey	-nut, s
monotonous	ly, ness
monster	s
month	s
monthl y	ies
monument	s
mood	s
mood y	ier, iest, ily, iness
moon	beam, less, light, s
moor	hen, land, s
moor	age, ed, ing, s
mop	ped, ping, per, head, s
moral	ly, s
more	over
morning* (a.m.)	s
morsel	s
mortal	ly, s
mortar	-board, s
mosaic	s

℮ Drop e before adding ing

*	missed	moan	morning
	mist	mown	mourning

mu   my

mosquito	*es*
moss	*es*
moss *y*	*ier, iest, iness*
most	*ly*
motel	*s*
moth	*-eaten, -proof, ball, s*
mother	*ed, ing, less, ly, hood, s*
motion	*ed, ing, less, -picture, s*
motor	*ed, ing, -bike, -boat, -car, ist, s*
motor	*-cycle, -cyclist, -scooter, way, s*
motto	*es*
mould	*ed, ing, er, s*
mould *y*	*ier, iest, iness*
moult	*ed, ing, s*
mound	*s*
mount	*ed, ing, s*
mountain	*ous, side, -top, s*
mountaineer	*ing, s*
mourn *ing* * (sorrowing)	*ed, ful, fully, er, s*
mouse *d, éing, éy, r, -hole, trap.* **mice**
moustache	*s*
mouth	*-organ, ful, s*
movable	*s*
move	*d, éing, r, ment, s*
mow	*ed, ing, er, s*
,mown * (cut grass, etc.)

mu

much	
mud	*-bank, -bath, -flat, guard*
mudd *y*	*ier, iest, ily, iness*
muddle	*d, éing, r, s*
muffle	*d, éing, r, s*
mulberr *y*	*ies*
mule	*teer, s*
multiplication	

multiply	*ing*
multipl *ied*	*ier, ies*
multitude	*s*
mumble	*d, éing, r, s*
mumm *y*	*ies*
mumps	
munch	*ed, ing, es*
mural	*s*
murder	*ed, ing, er, s*
murderess	*es*
murmur	*ed, ing, er, s*
muscle * (of body)	*s*
museum	*s*
mushroom	*s*
music	*al, ally, -case, -hall, -stand*
musician	*s*
musket	*eer, -shot, s*
mussel * (shellfish)	*s*
must	
mustn't (must not)	
mustard	*-pot*
must *y*	*ier, iest, ily, iness*
mutineer	*s*
mutiny	*ing*
mutin *ied*	*ies*
mutter	*ed, ing, er, s*
mutton	*-chop, -cutlet*
muzzle	*d, éing, s*

my

myrrh	
myself	
myster *y*	*ies*
mysterious	*ly, ness*
mystify	*ing*
mystif *ied*	*ies*

*é Drop **e** before adding ing*

*	mourning	mown	muscle
	morning	moan	mussel

na

nail *ed, ing, -scissors, -file, s*
naked *ly, ness*
name *d, ₑing, ly, less, -plate, sake, s*
nanny *ies*
napkin *-ring, s*
nappy *ies*
narcissus *es* or **narcissi**
narrate *d, ₑing, s*
narrow *ed, ing, er, est, ish, ly, ness, s*
nasturtium · *s*
nasty *ier, iest, ily, iness*
nation *al, ally, wide, s*
nationality *ies*
native *s*
nativity *ies*
natural *ly, ness*
naturalist *s*
nature *s*
naughty *ier, iest, ily, iness*
nautical *ly*
naval
nave* (main part of church) *s*
navigate *d, ₑing, s*
navigation
navigator *s*
navy *ies*

ne

near *ed, ing, er, est, ly, ness, s*
neat *er, est, ly, ness*
necessary *ily, ies*
necessity *ies*
neck *lace, let, line, tie, s*
need* (want) *ed, ing, s*
needn't (need not)

needle *work, -case, s*
negative *s*
neglect *ed, ing, s*
neglectful *ly, ness*
Negress *es*
Negro *es*
neigh *ed, ing, s*
neighbour *ing, ly, hood, s*
neither
nephew *s*
nerve *d, ₑing, -racking, s*
nervous *ly, ness*
nest *ed, ing, -egg, ful, s*
nestle *d, ₑing, s*
net *ted, ting, ball, ful, s*
nettle *s*
neutral *s*
never *more, theless*
new* (just made) *er, est, ly, ness*
news *caster, -letter, -reel, -sheet, y*
newsagent *s*
newspaper *man, men, -boy, -girl, s*
newt *s*
next

ni

nibble *d, ₑing, r, s*
nice *r, st, ly, ness*
nick *ed, ing, s*
nickname *d, ₑing, s*
niece *s*
night* *-club, fall, -light, mare, -time, s*
nightingale *s*
nil
nimble *r, st, ness, -footed*
nimbly

*ₑ Drop **e** before adding ing*

*	nave	need	new	night
	knave	knead	knew	knight

no	
no* (not any; opp. of yes)	es
noble	r, st, man, men, s
nobody	ies
nod	ded, ding, der, s
noise	less, lessly, s
noisy	ier, iest, ily, iness
nomad	ic, s
none* (not any)	
nonsense	
noodle	s
noon	day
noose	s
normal	ly
Norman	s
north	-east, -west, ern, erly, wards
nose	d, ∉ing, bag, bleed, dive, gay, s
nostril	s
not* (no)	
notable	s
notch	ed, ing, es
note	d, ∉ing, book, case, paper, let, s
nothing	
notice	d, ∉ing, able, ably, -board, s
notify	ing
notified	ication, ies
notion	s
nougat	
nought	s
nourish	ment, ed, ing, es
novel	ist, s
novelty	ies
November	s
novice	s
now	adays
nowhere	
nozzle	s

nu	
nuclear	
nude	s
nudist	s
nudge	d, ∉ing, s
nugget	s
nuisance	s
numb	ed, ing, ly, ness, s
number	ed, ing, -plate, s
numeral	s
numerical	ly
numerous	ly
nun* (religious woman)	s
nurse	d, ∉ing, maid, s
nursery	ies
nut	ted, ting, cracker, shell, -tree, s
nutty	ier, iest, ily, iness
nuthatch	es
nutmeg	s
nutrition	al, ist
nutritious	ly, ness
nuzzle	d, ∉ing, s

ny	
nylon	s
nymph	s

oa	
oaf* (stupid person)	ish, s or **oaves**
oak	-apple, -tree, s
oar* (rowing blade)	sman, smen, s
oasis	es
oast	-house, s
oat	meal, cake, s
oath* (promise; swear-word)	s

∉ Drop **e** before adding *ing*

*	no	none	not	oaf	oar
	know	nun	knot	oath	ore
					or

ob

obedience	
obedient	*ly*
obey	*ed, ing, s*
object	*ed, ing, or, s*
objection	*able, ably, s*
obligation	*s*
oblige	*d, ǿing, s*
obliterate	*d, ǿing, s*
oblong	*s*
oboe	*ǿist, s*
obscure	*d, ǿing, ly, s*
obscurity	
observant	*ly*
observation	*s*
observator y	*ies*
observe	*d, ǿing, r, s*
obstacle	*-course, -race, s*
obstinate	*ly*
obstruct	*ed, ing, ion, s*
obtain	*able, ed, ing, s*
obvious	*ly, ness*

oc

occasion	*al, ally, s*
occupant	*s*
occupation	*s*
occupy	*ing*
occup *ied*	*ier, ies*
occur	*red, ring, rence, s*
ocean	*s*
o'clock	
octagon	*al, s*
October	*s*
octopus	*es* or **octopodes**
oculist	*s*

od

odd	*er, est, ly, ness, ment, s*
odious	*ly, ness*
odour	*s*

of

of	
off	*ing, hand, chance, -side, spring*
offence	*s*
offend	*ed, ing, er, s*
offensive	*ly, ness*
offer	*ed, ing, s*
offertor y	*ies*
office	*-block, -boy, -girl, -worker, s*
officer	*s*
official	*ly, s*
often	*er, est*

og

ogre	*s*
ogress	*es*

oi

oil	*ed, ing, can, -rig, -stove, -well, s*
oil	*-heater, -painting, skin, -tanker, s*
oil y	*ier, iest, ily, iness*
ointment	*s*

ol

old	*en, er, est, ish, -time*
old-fashioned	*ness*
olive	*-oil, -grove, -tree, s*
Olympic Games or **Olympics**	

*ǿ Drop **e** before adding ing*

om on op   or os ot

om	
omelet(te)	s
omen	s
omission	s
omit	ted, ting, s
omnibus	es

on	
once	
oncoming	
one*	self, -sided, s
onion	y, -skin, s
onlooker	s
only	
onslaught	s
onto	
onward	s

op	
opal	s
opaque	ly, ness
open	ed, ing, ly, ness, er, s
opera	-glasses, -house, -singer, s
operatic	s
operate	d, ǿing, s
operation	s
operator	s
opinion	s
opponent	s
opportunit y	ies
oppose	d, ǿing, s
opposite	ly, ness
opposition	
optician	s
optimist	ic, ically, s

or	
oral	ly
orange	ade, -blossom, -peel, -tree, s
orang-(o)utan	s
orator	s
orbit	ed, ing, s
orchard	s
orchestra	l, s
orchid	s
ordeal	s
order	ed, ing, s
orderl y	iness, ies
ordinar y	ily, iness
ore* (metal in rock)	s
organ	-grinder, -loft, -pipe, ist, s
organization	s
organize	d, ǿing, r, s
orient	
oriental	s
origin	s
original	ity, ly
originate	d, ǿing, s
ornament	ed, ing, al, ation, s
ornithologist	s
ornithology	
orphan	ed, ing, age, s

os	
osier	s
ostrich	es

ot	
other	s
otherwise	
otter	s

ǿ Drop **e** before adding *ing*

*	one (1)	ore
	won	oar
		or

ou

ought
ounce *s*
our* (belonging to us) *s*
ourselves
out *come, let, look, put, right, standing*
outbreak *s*
outburst *s*
outcast *s*
outer *most*
outfit *ted, ting, ter, s*
outhouse *s*
outing *s*
outlaw *ed, ing, s*
outline *d, ɇing, s*
outnumber *ed, ing, s*
out-patient *s*
outpost *s*
outrage *d, ɇing, s*
outrageous *ly, ness*
outside *r, s*
outskirts
outward *ly, ness, s*
outwit *ted, ting, s*

ov

oval *s*
oven *s*
over *s*
overall *s*
overbalance *d, ɇing, s*
overboard
overcame
overcome *ɇing, s*
overcoat *s*
overcrowd *ed, ing, s*
overdose *d, ɇing, s*
overflow *ed, ing, s*
overhaul *ed, ing, s*
overhead *s*
overhear *ing, s*
overheard
overjoyed
overlap *ped, ping, s*
overload *ed, ing, s*
overlook *ed, ing, s*
overpower *ed, ing, s*
overseas
oversleep *ing, s*
overslept
overtake *n, ɇing, s*
overtook
overthrow *n, ing, s*
overthrew
overtime
overturn *ed, ing, s*
overwhelm *ed, ing, s*
overwork *ed, ing, s*

ow

owe *d, ɇing, s*
owl *et, s*
own *ed, ing, er, s*

ox

ox *en*
oxlip *s*
oxygen

oy

oyster *-bed, -catcher, -farm, -shell, s*

ɇ Drop **e** before adding *ing*

* our
hour

pa

pa	
pace	d, ¢ing, r, s
Pacific	
pack	ed, ing, er, s
package	d, ¢ing, s
packet	ed, ing, s
pad	ded, ding, der, s
paddle	d, ¢ing, r, -boat, -steamer, s
padlock	ed, ing, s
page	-boy, s
pageant	s
paid	
pail* (bucket)	ful, s
pain* (suffering)	ed, ing, -killer, s
painful	ly, ness
painless	ly, ness
paint	ed, ing, er, s
pair* (two)	ed, ing, s
palace	s
pale* (faint; whitish)	r, st, ly, ness, s
palette	s
palm	-tree, s
pamper	ed, ing, er, s
pamphlet	s
pan	ned, ning, ful, cake, s
panda	s
pane* (sheet of glass)	s
panel	led, ling, list, s
panic	ked, king, ky, -stricken, -struck, s
panorama	s
pans y	ies
pant	ed, ing, s
panther	s
pantomime	s
pantr y	ies
paper	ed, ing, -boy, -girl, -chain, -clip, s
papier mâché	

parachute	d, ¢ing, -troops, s
parade	d, ¢ing, -ground, s
paraffin	-heater, -oil
parallel	ed, ing, s
paralyse	d, ¢ing, s
paralys is	es
paratroops	
parcel	led, ling, s
parch	ed, ing, es
parchment	s
pardon	able, ed, ing, s
pare* (cut away; peel)	d, ¢ing, s
parent	age, al, s
parish	es
park	ed, ing, land, -keeper, s
parliament	s
parrot	s
parsley	-sauce
parsnip	s
parson	age, s
part	ed, ing, ly, s
particle	s
particular	ly, s
partition	ed, ing, s
partner	ed, ing, ship, s
partridge	s
part y	ies
pass	ed*, ing, able, es
passage	way, s
passenger	s
passion	ate, ately, s
passport	s
password	s
past* (time gone by)	
paste	d, ¢ing, s
pastel* (crayon)	led, ling, s
pastille* (sweet)	s

¢ Drop e before adding ing

	pail	pain	pair		passed	pastel
*	pale	pane	pare		past	pastille
			pear			

pe

pastime	s
pastr y	ies
pasture	d, ǿing, s
past y	ies
pat	ted, ting, s
patch	ed, ing, work, es
patch y	ier, iest, ily, iness
path	way, s
pathetic	ally
patience	
patient	ly, s
patrol	led, ling, man, men, -leader, s
patter	· ed, ing, s
pattern	ed, ing, -book, s
pause* (hesitate)	d, ǿing, s
pave	d, ǿing, ment, s
pavilion	s
paw (animal's foot)	s,* ed, ing
pawn	ed, ing, broker, shop, -ticket, s
pay	able, ing, er, ment, -day, -desk, s
paid	

pe

pea	nut, -pod, -soup, -shooter, s
peace* (quiet)	able, -offering, -time
peaceful	ly, ness
peach	es
peacock	s
peahen	s
peak	ed, ing, s
peal* (sound of bells)	ed, ing, s
pear* (fruit)	-drop, -tree, s
pearl	-diver, -fisher, s
peasant	ry, s
peat	-bog, -moor, y
pebble	-stone, s
pebbl y	ier, iest, iness

peck	ed, ing, er, s
peculiar	ly
peculiarit y	ies
pedal* (foot-lever)	led, ling, -cycle, s
peddle* (to hawk goods)	d, ǿing, s
pedestrian	s
pedigree	s
pedlar	s
peel* (skin of fruit)	ed, ing, er, s
peep	ed, ing, er, -hole, -show, s
peer* (stare)	ed, ing, s
peg	ged, ging, s
Pekin(g)ese	Pekin(g)ese
pelican	s
pellet	s
pelt	ed, ing, s
pen	ned, ning, -friend, -nib, s
penalt y	ies
pence	
pencil	led, ling, -case, -sharpener, s
pendulum	s
penetrate	d, ǿing, s
penguin	s
peninsula	s
pen knife	knives
pennant	s
penn y	ies or **pence**
penniless	ly, ness
pension	ed, ing, able, er, -book, s
people	s
pepper	ed, ing, y, -pot, mint, s
perambulator	s
perch	ed, ing, es
percussion	-band, s
perfect	ly, ed, ing, ion, s
perform	ed, ing, ance, er, s
perfume	d, ǿing, s

ǿ Drop **e** before adding *ing*

*	pause	peace	pear	peal	pedal	peer
	paws	piece	pair	peel	peddle	pier
			pare			

ph   pi

perhaps	
peril	*ous, ously, s*
period	*ic, ical, ically, s*
periscope	*s*
perish	*ed, ing, es*
permanent	*ly*
permission	
permit	*ted, ting, s*
perplex	*ed, ing, es*
persevere	*d, e̸ing, e̸ance, s*
persist	*ed, ing, ence, ent, s*
person	*al, ally, s*
perspiration	
perspire	*d, e̸ing, s*
persuade	*d, e̸ing, s*
persuasion	
persuasive	*ly, ness*
pessimist	*ic, ically, s*
pester	*ed, ing, s*
pet	*ted, ting, -shop, s*
petal	*s*
petrol	*eum, -pump, -station, s*
petticoat	*s*
pew	*s*
pewter	

ph

phantom	*s*
pheasant	*s*
philatelist	*s*
phone	*d, e̸ing, -booth, s*
photo	*-fit, -frame, s*
photograph	*ed, ing, y, er, s*
physical	*ly*
physician	*s*
physics	

pi

pi* ($\pi = 3.14159$)	
pianist	*s*
piano	*-accordion, -stool, s*
piccolo	*-player, s*
pick *ed, ing, er, axe, pocket, s*	
pickle	*d, e̸ing, r, s*
picnic *ked, king, ker, -basket, s*	
picture	*d, e̸ing, -book, -frame, s*
picturesque	*ly, ness*
pie*	*crust, -shop, s*
piece* (a part)	*d, e̸ing, s*
pier* (jetty)	*s*
pierce	*d, e̸ing, s*
pierrot	*s*
pig	*let, skin, s*
pigst *y*	*ies*
pigeon	*-hole, -house, -loft, s*
pigm *y* or **pygm** *y*	*ies*
pigtail	*s*
pike	*man, men, staff, s*
pilchard	*s*
pile	*d, e̸ing, s*
pilgrim	*age, s*
pillar	*s*
pillar-box	*es*
pillion	*-rider, -seat, s*
pillow	*case, slip, -fight, s*
pilot	*ed, ing, s*
pimple	*d, e̸ing, s*
pimpl *y*	*ier, iest, iness*
pin	*ned, ning, cushion, s*
pincers	**pincers**
pinch	*ed, ing, es*
pine *d, e̸ing, apple, -cone, -needle, -tree, s*	
pink	*er, est, ish, y, ness, s*
pint	*s*

e̸ Drop **e** before adding *ing*

* pi	piece	pier
pie	peace	peer

pl

pioneer	ed, ing, s
pipe	d, ∉ing, r, -cleaner, ful, s
piranha	s
pirate	s
pistil* (part of flower)	s
pistol* (small gun)	-shot, s
pit	ted, ting, fall, -head, -prop, s
pitch	ed, ing, -black, -dark, es
pitchfork	ed, ing, s
piteous	ly
pity	ing
pitied	iful, iless, ies
pixie	s or **pix**y, ies
pizza	s

pl

placard	s
place* (position)	d, ing, s
plague	d, ∉ing, s
plaice* (fish)	**plaice**
plain*	er, est, ly, ness, s
plait	ed, ing, s
plan	ned, ning, ner, s
plane* (tool; to smooth)	d, ∉ing, s
plane* (aeroplane; tree)	s
planet	s
plank	ed, ing, s
plant	ed, ing, ation, er, s
plaster	ed, ing, er, s
plastic	s
plasticine	
plate	d, ∉ing, ful, -glass, -rack, s
platform	s
platinum	
play	ed, ing, ground, mate, time, er, s
play	-group, -pen, thing, wright, s
playful	ly, ness

po

plead	ed, ing, s
pleasant	ly, ness
please	d, ∉ing, s
pleasure	s
pleat	ed, ing, s
plentiful	ly, ness
plenty	
pliers	**pliers**
plimsoll	s
plod	ded, ding, der, s
plot	ted, ting, ter, s
plough	ed, ing, man, men, boy, s
pluck	ed, ing, er, s
plucky	ier, iest, ily, iness
plug	ged, ging, ger, s
plum*	-pudding, -stone, -tree, s
plumage	
plumb*	ed, ing, -line, s
plumber	s
plump	er, est, ly, ness
plunder	ed, ing, er, s
plunge	d, ∉ing, r, s
plural	s
plus	es

po

poach	ed, ing, es
poacher	s
pocket	ed, ing, -book, -money, ful, s
pocket-knife	-knives
podgy	ier, iest, ily, iness
poem	s
poet	ic, ical, ically, s
poetry	
point	ed, ing, -blank, -duty, less, er,'s
poise	d, ∉ing, s
poison	ed, ing, ous, ously, er, s

∉ Drop **e** before adding *ing*

*	pistil	place	plain	plum
	pistol	plaice	plane	plumb

poke	d, ǿing, r, s	**portable**	s
polar bear	s	**porter**	s
pole* (long rod)	-jump, -vault, s	**porthole**	s
police	d, ǿing, -officer, man, woman	**portion**	ed, ing, s
police force	s	**portrait**	s
police station	s	**pose**	d, ǿing, s
polish	ed, ing, es	**position**	ed, ing, s
polite	r, st, ly, ness	**positive**	ly, ness
political	ly	**possess**	ed, ing, ive, es
politician	s	**possession**	s
poll* (vote)	ed, ing, s	**possibilit**y	ies
pollen		**possible**	s
polo	-stick	**possibly**	
polytechnic	s	**post**	ed, ing, man, men, card, mark, s
polythene		**postage**	-stamp
pomp	ous, ously, osity	**postal order**	s
pond	-life, -snail, weed, s	**poster**	s
ponder	ed, ing, s	**post office**	s
pontoon	-bridge, s	**postpone**	d, ǿing, ment, s
pony	ies	**pos**y	ies
poodle	s	**pot**	ted, ting, ful, -luck, -hole, -shot, s
pool	ed, ing, s	**potato**	es
poor* (not rich)	er, est, ly, ness	**potion**	s
pop	ped, ping, per, corn, gun, s	**potter**	ed, ing, s
pop	-group, -music, -singer, -song, s	**potter**y.	ies
poplar	-tree, s	**pouch**	es
poppy	ies	**poultice**	d, ǿing, s
popular	ity, ly	**poultry**	-farm
population		**pounce**	d, ǿing, s
porcelain		**pound**	ed, ing, s
porch	es	**pour*** (flow out)	ed, ing, er, s
porcupine	s	**pout**	ed, ing, er, s
pore* (study; tiny hole)	d, ǿing, s	**poverty**	-stricken
pork	-butcher, -chop, -pie, er, y	**powder**	ed, ing, y, -puff, -room, s
porpoise	s	**power**	ed, -house, -plant, -station, s
porridge		**powerful**	ly, ness
port	s	**powerless**	ly, ness

ǿ Drop **e** before adding *ing*

*	pole	poor
	poll	pore
		pour

pr_a pre   pri   pro

pr

practical	*ly, ity, ness*
practice* (noun)	*s*
practise* (verb)	*d, ȩing, s*
prairie	*s*
praise	*d, ȩing, s*
prance	*d, ȩing, s*
prank	*ster, s*
prawn	*ed, ing, er, s*
pray* (ask God)	*ed, ing, s*
prayer	*-book, -meeting, s*
preach	*ed, ing, es*
preacher	*s*
precaution	*ary, s*
precious	*ly, ness*
precipice	*s*
prefect	*s*
prefer	*red, ring, able, ably, ence, s*
prehistoric	*al, ally*
preliminar *y*	*ies*
premises	
preparation	*s*
prepare	*d, ȩing, s*
prescribe	*d, ȩing, s*
prescription	*s*
presence	
present	*ed, ing, ation, s*
presently	
preserve	*d, ȩing, s*
president	*s*
press	*ed, ing, es*
pressure	*-cooker, -gauge, s*
pretend	*ed, ing, er, s*
prett *y*	*ier, iest, ily, iness*
prevent	*ed, ing, ion, s*
previous	*ly, ness*
prey* (victim; thing hunted)	*ed, ing, s*

price	*d, ȩing, less, -list, -tag, s*
prick	*ed, ing, er, s*
prickle	*d, ȩing, s*
prickl *y*	*ier, iest, iness*
pride* (proudness)	*d, ȩing, s*
pried* (looked into)	
priest	*ly, hood, s*
priestess	*es*
primary school	*s*
primitive	*ly, ness*
primrose	*s*
prince	*ly, s*
princess	*es*
principal* (head; chief)	*ly, s*
principle* (rule; truth)	*s*
print	*ed, ing, er, s*
prison	*er, s*
private	*ly, s*
privilege	*d, ȩing, s*
prize	*d, ȩing, -winner, s*
probabilit *y*	*ies*
probable	*s*
probably	
problem	*s*
procedure	*s*
proceed	*ed, ing, s*
process	*ed, ing, es*
procession	*s*
proclaim	*ed, ing, s*
procure	*d, ȩing, s*
prod	*ded, ding, s*
produce	*d, ȩing, r, s*
product	*ive, ion, s*
profession	*al, ally, s*
professor	*s*
profit* (gain)	*able, ed, ing, eer, s*
programme	*d, ȩing, r, s*

ȩ Drop **e** before adding *ing*

*	practice	pray		pride	principal	profit
	practise	prey		pried	principle	prophet

progress	*ed, ing, es*	**pu**	
prohibit	*ed, ing, s*	**public**	*ly, -house*
project *ed, ing, ile, ion, or, s*		**publication**	*s*
promenade	*d, ǿing, r, s*	**publicity**	
prominent	*ly*	**publish**	*ed, ing, es*
promise	*d, ǿing, s*	**publisher**	*s*
promote	*d, ǿing, r, s*	**pudding**	*s*
promotion	*s*	**puddle**	*s*
prompt *ed, ing, er, est, ly, ness, s*		**puff**	*ed, ing, er, s*
pronounce	*d, ǿing, ment, s*	**puff** *y*	*ier, iest, ily, iness*
proof	*s*	**pull**	*ed, ing, er, s*
prop	*ped, ping, s*	**pullover**	*s*
propel	*led, ling, ler, s*	**pulley**	*-block, s*
proper	*ly*	**pulp**	*ed, ing, er, s*
propert *y*	*ies*	**pulpit**	*s*
prophec *y* (noun)	*ies*	**pulse**	*d, ǿing, s*
prophes *y* (verb)	*ied, ies*	**pump**	*ed, ing, s*
prophesying		**pumpkin**	*s*
prophet* (foreteller of future) *s*		**punch**	*ed, ing, es*
proposal	*s*	**punctual**	*ity, ly*
propose	*d, ǿing, r, s*	**puncture**	*d, ǿing, s*
proprietor	*s*	**punish**	*able, ed, ing, es*
prosecute	*d, ǿing, s*	**punishment**	*s*
prosper *ed, ing, ous, ously, ity, s*		**punt**	*ed, ing, er, s*
protect *ed, ing, ion, ive, or, s*		**pupa**	*e*
protest	*ed, ing, s*	**pupil**	*s*
Protestant	*s*	**puppet**	*ry, -play, -show, s*
protrude	*d, ǿing, s*	**pupp** *y*	*ies*
proud	*er, est, ly*	**purchase**	*d, ǿing, r, s*
prove	*d, ǿing, s*	**pure**	*r, st, ly, ness*
proverb	*s*	**purity**	
provide	*d, ǿing, r, s*	**purple**	*r, st, ness, s*
provision	*ed, ing, s*	**purpose**	*ly, s*
prowl	*ed, ing, er, s*	**purr**	*ed, ing, s*
prune	*d, ǿing, s*	**purse**	*r, -snatcher, s*
pry	*ing*	**pursue**	*d, ǿing, r, s*
pr *ied* ***	*ies*	**pursuit**	*s*

ǿ Drop **e** before adding *ing*

*	prophet	pried
	profit	pride

push	ed, ing, es
puss y	ies
put	ting, s
putt (golf)	ed, ing, er, s
putting-green	s
putty	
puzzle	d, ǿing, r, ment, s

py

pygm y or **pigm** y	ies
pyjamas	
pylon	s
pyramid	s
python	s

qua

quack	ed, ing, s
quadrangle	s
quadruplet	s
quaint	er, est, ly, ness
quake	d, ǿing, s
qualification	s
qualify	ing
qualif ied	ies
qualit y	ies
quantit y	ies
quarantine	d, ǿing, s
quarrel	led, ling, ler, some, s
quarry	ing
quarr ied	ies
quart (two pints)	s*
quarter	ed, ing, s
quartet(te)	s
quartz* (rock-crystal)	
quay* (wharf)	side, s

que

queen	s
queer	er, est, ly, ness
quell	ed, ing, s
quench	ed, ing, es
query	ing
quer ied	ies
quest	ed, ing, s
question	ed, ing, er, -master, s
queue* (line of persons, etc.)	d, r, s
queueing or **queuing**	

qui

quibble	d, ǿing, r, s
quick	er, est, ly, ness
quicken	ed, ing, s
quiet	ed, ing, er, est, ly, ness, s
quieten	ed, ing, s
quill	s
quilt	ed, ing, s
quince	s
quinine	
quintet(te)	s
quintuplet	s
quire* (measure of paper)	s
quit	ted, ting, ter, s
quite	
quiver	ed, ing, s
quiz	zed, zing, zes

quo

quoit	s
quota	s
quotation	-mark, s
quote	d, ǿing, s

ǿ Drop **e** before adding *ing*

*	quarts	quay	queue	quire
	quartz	key	cue	choir

ra   re_a

ra

rabbit	*ed, ing, er, -hole, -warren, s*
race	*d, ǿing, r, course, horse, track, s*
rack	*ed, ing, s*
racket* (noise)	*ed, ing, eer, s*
racket* or **racquet*** (bat)	*s*
radar	
radiate	*d, ǿing, s*
radiator	*s*
radio	*ed, ing, s*
radish	*es*
radi*us*	*i*
raffle	*d, ǿing, r, -ticket, s*
raft	*s*
rafter	*s*
rag	*ged, ging, s*
ragged	*ly, ness*
rage	*d, ǿing, s*
raid	*ed, ing, er, s*
rail	*ing, s*
railway	*-carriage, -crossing, -line, s*
rain*	*ed, ing, -water, bow, coat, drop, s*
rain*y*	*ier, iest, ily, iness*
raise* (lift up)	*d, ǿing, s*
raisin	*s*
rake	*d, ǿing, r, s*
rally	*ing*
rall*ied*	*ies*
ram	*med, ming, rod, s*
ramble	*d, ǿing, r, s*
ramshackle	
ranch	*es*
rancher	*s*
random	*ly*
rang	
range	*d, ǿing, r, s*
rank	*ed, ing, s*

ransack	*ed, ing, er, s*
ransom	*ed, ing, s*
rap* (knock)	*ped, ping, s*
rapid	*ity, ly, s*
rare	*r, st, ly, ness*
rascal	*ly, s*
rash	*er, est, ly, ness*
rasher	*s*
raspberr*y*	*ies*
rat	*ted, ting, -hole, -poison, -trap, s*
rate	*d, ǿing, payer, s*
rather	
ration	*ed, ing, s*
rattle	*d, ǿing, r, snake, s*
rave	*d, ǿing, s*
raven	*s*
ravenous	*ly, ness*
ravine	*s*
raw	*er, est, ly, ness*
ray (beam of light)	*s**
razor	*-blade, -edge, -shell, s*

re

reach	*ed, ing, es*
react	*ed, ing, ion, or, s*
read*	*ing, er, s*
read*y*	*ier, iest, ily, iness*
real* (true)	*ly, ist, istic, ism*
realit*y*	*ies*
realize	*d, ǿing, s*
really	
reap	*ed, ing, er, s*
reappear	*ed, ing, ance, s*
rear	*ed, ing, guard, -lamp, -light, ward, s*
rearrange	*d, ǿing, ment, s*
reason	*ed, ing, able, ably, s*

ǿ Drop **e** before adding *ing*

racket	rain	raise	rap	read	read	real
racquet	reign	rays	wrap	reed	red	reel
	rein					

rebel	led, ling, s	**refer**	red, ring, s
rebellion	s	**referee**	d, ing, s
rebellious	ly, ness	**reference**	-book, s
rebound	ed, ing, s	**reflect**	ed, ing, ion, or, s
recall	ed, ing, s	**refrain**	ed, ing, s
recapture	d, ∉ing, s	**refresh**	ed, ing, es
receipt	ed, ing, -book, s	**refreshment**	s
receive	d, ∉ing, r, s	**refrigerator**	s
recent	ly, ness	**refuge**	s
receptacle	s	**refugee**	s
reception	ist, s	**refund**	ed, ing, s
recess	ed, ing, es	**refusal**	s
recipe	s	**refuse**	d, ∉ing, s
recital	s	**regain**	ed, ing, s
recitation	s	**regard**	ed, ing, less, lessly, s
recite	d, ∉ing, s	**regatta**	s
reckless	ly, ness	**regiment**	ed, ing, al, s
reckon	ed, ing, er, s	**region**	al, s
recognize	d, ∉ing, s	**register**	ed, ing, s
recollect	ed, ing, ion, s	**regret**	ted, ting, table, tably, s
recommend	ed, ing, ation, s	**regretful**	ly
record	ed, ing, -player, s	**regular**	ity, ly
recorder	s	**regulate**	d, ∉ing, s
recover	ed, ing, s	**regulation**	s
recovery	ies	**rehearsal**	s
recreation	-ground, s	**rehearse**	d, ∉ing, s
recruit	ed, ing, ment, s	**reign*** (rule)	ed, ing, s
rectangle	s	**rein*** (strap)	ed, ing, s
red* (colour)	der, dest, dish, dy, ness, s	**reindeer**	reindeer
redden	ed, ing, s	**reinforce**	d, ∉ing, ment, s
redskin	s	**reject**	ed, ing, ion, s
redecorate	d, ∉ing, s	**rejoice**	d, ∉ing, s
reduce	d, ∉ing, s	**rejoin**	ed, ing, s
reduction	s	**relate**	d, ∉ing, s
reed* (tall grass)	s	**relation**	s
reef	-knot, s	**relative**	s
reel* (spool; dance; stagger)	ed, ing, s	**relax**	ed, ing, es

∉ Drop **e** before adding *ing*

* red   reed   reel   reign
  read   read   real   rein
                             rain

rem **ren** **rep** **req** **res** **ret** **rev** **rew**

relay	ed, ing, -race, s		**request**	ed, ing, s
release	d, øing, s		**require**	d, øing, ment, s
reliable	ness		**rescue**	d, øing, r, s
relic	s		**resemblance**	s
relief			**resemble**	d, øing, s
relieve	d, øing, s		**reservation**	s
religion	s		**reserve**	d, øing, s
religious	ly, ness		**reservoir**	s
rely	ing		**reside**	d, øing, nce, nt, s
relied	iable, ies		**resign**	ed, ing, ation, s
remain	ed, ing, der, s		**resist**	ed, ing, ance, s
remark	ed, ing, able, ably, s		**resolution**	s
remedy	ies		**resort**	ed, ing, s
remember	ed, ing, s		**respect**	ed, ing, able, ably, ful, fully, s
remembrance	s		**responsibilit**y	ies
remind	ed, ing, er, s		**responsible**	
remnant	s		**rest**	ed, ing, -cure, -home, -room, s
remote	ly, ness		**restful**	ly, ness
removal	s		**restless**	ly, ness
remove	d, øing, r, s		**restaurant**	s
renew	ed, ing, able, al, s		**result**	ed, ing, s
rent	ed, ing, able, al, s		**resume**	d, øing, s
repair	ed, ing, able, er, s		**retire**	d, øing, ment, s
repay	ing, able, ment, s		**retrace**	d, øing, s
repaid			**retreat**	ed, ing, s
repeat	ed, edly, ing, er, s		**retrieve**	d, øing, r, s
repetition	s		**return**	ed, ing, able, -ticket, s
replace	d, øing, able, ment, s		**reveal**	ed, ing, s
replay	ed, ing, s		**revenge**	d, øing, s
reply	ing		**reverse**	d, øing, s
replied	ies		**review**	ed, ing, s
report	ed, ing, er, s		**revive**	d, øing, s
represent	ed, ing, ative, s		**revolt**	ed, ing, s
reproduce	d, øing, s		**revolution**	s
reptile	s		**revolve**	d, øing, s
republic	an, s		**revolver**	s
reputation	s		**reward**	ed, ing, s

ø Drop **e** before adding *ing*

rh   ri   ro

rh	
rheumatism	
rhinoceros	es
rhododendron	s
rhubarb	
rhyme	d, ẹing, s
rhythm	ic, ical, ically, s

ri	
rib	bed, bing, s
ribbon	s
rice	-pudding, -field, s
rich	er, est, ly, ness, es
rick	ed, ing, s
ricket y	iness
ridden	
riddle	d, ẹing, r, s
ride	ẹing, r, s
riding	-crop, -school, -stable, -whip, s
ridge	s
ridicule	d, ẹing, s
ridiculous	ly, ness
rifle	d, ẹing, man, men, -range, -shot, s
rig	ged, ging, ger, s
right* (true; opp. left)	ful, ly, -handed, s
rigid	ity, ly, ness
rim	med, ming, less, s
rind	s
ring* (circle)	ed, ing, leader, -master, s
ring* (bell sound)	ing, er, s
rink	s
rinse	d, ẹing, r, s
riot	ed, ing, er, s
rip	ped, ping, per, -cord, s
ripe	r, st, ly, ness
ripen	ed, ing, s

ripple	d, ẹing, s
rise	ẹing, r, s
risen	
risk	ed, ing, s
risk y	ier, iest, ily, iness
rissole	s
rival	led, ling, s
rivalr y	ies
river	-bank, -bed, -boat, side, s
rivet	ed, ing, er, s

ro	
road* (highway)	side, way, -sweeper, s
roam	ed, ing, er, s
roar	ed, ing, er, s
roast	ed, ing, er, s
rob	bed, bing, ber, s
robber y	ies
robe	d, ẹing, s
robin	-redbreast, s
robot	s
rock	ed, ing, -cake, -garden, s
rock y	ier, iest, ily, iness
rocker y	ies
rocket	ed, ing, s
rode* (ride)	
rodeo	s
roe* (deer; fish eggs)	s
rogue	s
rôle* (actor's part)	s
roll* (turn over)	ed, ing, -call, mop, er, s
roller-skate	d, ẹing, r, s
Roman	s
romance	d, ẹing, s
romantic	ally, s
romp	ed, ing, er, s

ẹ Drop **e** before adding *ing*

*	right	ring		road	roe	rôle
	write	wring		rode	row	roll
				rowed		

ru　　　　　　sa

roof	-garden, -rack, -top, s
rook	s
rooker y	ies
room	ful, s
room y	ier, iest, ily, iness
root* (part of a plant)	ed, ing, s
rope	d, ǿing, -ladder, s
rose	-bud, -garden, -hip, -tree, wood, s
rosette	s
ros y	ier, iest, ily, iness
rot	ted, ting, s
rotate	d, ǿing, s
rotten	ly, ness
rough	ed, ing, er, est, ly, ness, s
roughen	ed, ing, s
round	ed, ing, ish, ness, sman, smen, s
roundabout	s
rounders	
rouse	d, ǿing, s
route* (a way)	d, ǿing, s
routine	s
rove	d, ǿing, r, s
row (quarrel)	ed, ing, s
row* (line; use oars)	ed,* ing, er, -boat, s
rowing-boat	s
rowd y	ier, iest, ily, iness, ies
royal	ist, ly, ty

ru

rub	bed, bing, s
rubber	-stamp, -tree, s
rubbish	-tip, -heap, y
rubble	
rub y	ies
rucksack	s
rudder	s

rude	r, st, ly, ness
ruffian	s
ruffle	d, ǿing, s
Rugby	-ball
rugged	ly, ness
ruin	ed, ing, ous, s
rule	d, ǿing, r, s
rumble	d, ǿing, s
rummage	d, ǿing, -sale, s
rumour	ed, ing, s
run	ning, ner, way, s
rung* (ring; ladder step)	s
rural	ly, ness
rush	ed, ing, es
rust	ed, ing, less, -proof, s
rust y	ier, iest, ily, iness
rustle	d, ǿing, r, s
rut	ted, ting, s
rutt y	ier, iest, iness

sa

sabbath	s
sack	ed, ing, ful, -race, s
sacred	ly, ness
sacrifice	d, ǿing, s.
sad	der, dest, ly, ness
sadden	ed, ing, s
saddle	d, ǿing, r, -bag, s
safari	s
safe	r, st, ly, ness, s
safety	-catch, -lamp, -net, -pin, -valve
sag	ged, ging, s
sago	s
said	
sail* (travel by ship)	ed, ing, s
sailor	s

ǿ Drop **e** before adding *ing*

*	root	row	rowed	rung	sail
	route	roe	road	wrung	sale
			rode		

SC

saint	s		sauce	pan, s
saintl y	ier, iest, ily, iness		saucer	ful, s
sake	s		sauc y	ier, iest, ily, iness
salad	-dressing, -oil, s		saunter	ed, ing, s
salar y	ies		sausage	-meat, -roll, s
sale* (selling)	sman, smen, -room, s		savage	d, eing, ly, ry, ness, s
salmon	**salmon**		save	d, eing, s
saloon	s		saviour	s
salt	ed, ing, -water, -cellar, -spoon, s		saw	ed, ing, dust, mill, s
salt y	ier, iest, iness		sawn or **sawed**	
salute	d, eing, s		Saxon	s
salvage	d, eing, s		saxophone	s
same	ness		say	ing, s
sample	d, eing, r, s		said	
sanatorium	s or **sanatoria**			
sanctuar y	ies			
sand	-castle, -dune, paper, -storm, s			**SC**
sand y	ier, iest, iness		scabbard	s
sandal	s		scaffold	ing, s
sandwich	ed, ing, es		scald	ed, ing, s
sang			scale	d, eing, s
sank			scalp	ed, ing, s
Santa Claus			scamp	ed, ing, s
sap	ped, ping, ling, s		scamper	ed, ing, s
sapphire	s		scan	ned, ning, ner, s
sarcastic	ally		scar	red, ring, s
sardine	s		scarce	r, st, ly, ness
sash	es		scarcit y	ies
satchel	s		scare	d, eing, r, crow, s
satellite	s		scarf	-ring, s or **scarves**
satin	s		scarlet	s
satisfaction			scatter	ed, ing, -brain, s
satisfactor y	ily, iness		scavenge	d, eing, r, s
satisfy	ing		scene* (view; place)	-shifter, s
satisf ied	ies		scenery	
saturate	d, eing, s		scent* (smell; perfume)	ed, ing, s
Saturday	s		scheme	d, eing, r, s

e Drop **e** before adding *ing*

*	sale	scene	scent
	sail	seen	sent

scholar	ship, s
scholastic	ally
school	ed, ing, boy, girl, -teacher, s
schoolmaster	s
schoolmistress	es
schooner	s
science	-fiction, s
scientific	ally
scientist	s
scissors	**scissors**
scold	ed, ing, er, s
scone	s
scoop	ed, ing, er, s
scooter	s
scorch	ed, ing, es
score	d, éing, r, -board, -card, s
scorn	ed, ing, er, s
scornful	ly, ness
scorpion	s
scoundrel	s
scour	ed, ing, er, s
scout	ed, ing, er, master, s
scowl	ed, ing, er, s
scraggy	ier, iest, ily, iness
scramble	d, éing, r, s
scrap	ped, ping, py, -book, -heap, s
scrape	d, éing, r, s
scratch	ed, ing, es
scratchy	ier, iest, ily, iness
scrawl	ed, ing, er, s
scrawly	ier, iest, iness
scream	ed, ing, er, s
screech	ed, ing, es
screechy	ier, iest, ily, iness
screen	ed, ing, s
screw	ed, ing, driver, s
scribble	d, éing, r, s

scripture	s
scroll	s
scrub	bed, bing, ber, s
scrum	med, ming, mage, s
scuffle	d, éing, r, s
scull* (oar; to row)	ed, ing, er, s
scullery	ies
sculptor	s
sculptress	es
sculpture	d, éing, s
scuttle	d, éing, s
scythe	d, éing, s

se

sea*	side, sick, shore, front, port, s
sea*	-gull, -horse, -lion, -serpent, s
sea*	man, men, -shell, -water, weed, s
Sea Scout	s
seal	ed, ing, er, skin, s
sealing* (fastening)	-wax
seam* (join; rock vein)	less, s
search	ed, ing, es
searchlight	s
season	-ticket, s
seat	ed, ing, er, -belt, s
seclude	d, éing, s
second	ly, -class, -hand, -rate, s
secondary	
secrecy	
secret	ive, ly, s
secretary	ies
section	s
secure	d, éing, ly, ness, s
security	ies
see* (notice)	ing, s
seed	ed, ing, y, ling, -bed, -cake, s

é Drop **e** before adding *ing*

*	scull	sea	sealing	seam
	skull	see	ceiling	seem

seek	ing, er, s
seem* (appear)	ed, ing, s
seen* (noticed)	
see-saw	ed, ing, s
seize	d, ∉ing, s
seldom	
select	ed, ing, ion, s
self	-conscious, -service, selves
selfish	ly, ness
sell* (exchange for money)	ing, er,* s
sellotape	d, ∉ing, s
semicircle	s
semicircular	ly
semi-detached	
semolina	
send	ing, er, s
senior	s
sensation	al, ally, s
sense	d, ∉ing, s
senseless	ly, ness
sensible	ness
sensibly	
sent* (send)	
sentence	d, ∉ing, s
sentinel	s
sentry	ies
separate	d, ∉ing, ly, ness, s
separation	s
September	s
sequin	s
serenade	d, ∉ing, r, s
serf* (villein; slave)	dom, s
sergeant	-major, s
serial* (in parts—as story or film)	s
series	
serious	ly, ness
sermon	s

serpent	s
servant	-girl, s
serve	d, ∉ing, r, s
service	d, ∉ing, s
serviette	s
session	s
set	ting, ter, -square, s
settee	s
settle	d, ∉ing, r, ment, s
several	
severe	r, st, ly
severity	
sew* (stitch)	ed, ing, er, s
sewing-machine	s
sewn* (fastened with stitches)	
sextet(te)	s

sh

shabby	ier, iest, ily, iness
shack	s
shade	d, ∉ing, s
shady	ier, iest, ily, iness
shadow	ed, ing, s
shadowy	ily, iness
shaft	s
shaggy	ier, iest, ily, iness
shake	n, ∉ing, r, s
shaky	ier, iest, ily, iness
shall	
shallow	er, est, ly, ness, s
shamble	d, ∉ing, s
shame	d, ∉ing, s
shameful	ly, ness
shameless	ly, ness
shampoo	ed, ing, s
shamrock	s

∉ Drop e before adding ing

seem	seen	sell	seller	sent	serf	serial	sew	sewn
seam	scene	cell	cellar	scent	surf	cereal	sow, so	sown

shandy ies	**shingle** s
shan't (shall not)	**ship** ped, ping, load, mate, yard, s
shanty ies	**shipwreck** ed, ing, s
shape - d, ǿing, ly, s	**shirk** ed, ing, er, s
shapeless ly, ness	**shirt** -button, -sleeve, -tail, s
share d, ǿing, s	**shiver** ed, ing, y, s
shark skin, s	**shoal** ed, ing, s
sharp er, est, ly, ness, -shooter, s	**shock** ed, ing, s
sharpen ed, ing, er, s	**shodd**y ier, iest, ily, iness
shatter ed, ing, s	**shoe*** ing, -bag, horn, -lace, maker, s
shave n, d, ǿing, r, s	**shod**
shawl s	**shone**
sheaf **sheaves**	**shoo*** (frighten away) ed, ing, s
shear* (cut; clip) ed, ing, er, s	**shook**
sheath s	**shoot*** (fire) ing, er, s
sheath-knife -knives	**shop** ped, ping, per, keeper, lifter, s
shed ding, der, s	**shore*** (sea shore) s
sheep -dog, -farmer, -pen, skin, **sheep**	**shorn**
sheer* (steep)	**short** age, er, est, ly, ness, bread, s
sheet s	**shorten** ed, ing, s
sheik(h) s	**shorthand**
shelf **shelves**	**shot** -gun, s
shell ed, ing, er, s	**should**
shellfish es or **shellfish**	**shouldn't** (should not)
she'll (she will; she shall)	**shoulder** ed, ing, -bag, -blade, -strap, s
shelter ed, ing, s	**shout** ed, ing, er, s
shepherd s	**shovel** led, ling, ler, ful, s
shepherdess es	**show** n, ed, ing, -case, room, s
sherbet s	**show** -jumping, -ground, s
sheriff s	**shower** ed, ing, -bath, s
sherry ies	**shower**y ier, iest, iness
she's (she is; she has)	**shrank**
shield ed, ing, s	**shred** ded, ding, der, s
shift ed, ing, y, er, s	**shrewd** er, est, ly, ness
shin ned, ning, -guard, -pad, s	**shriek** ed, ing, er, s
shine ǿing, s	**shrill** ed, ing, er, est, y, ness, s
shiny ier, iest, ily, iness	**shrimp** ed, ing, er, s or **shrimp**

ǿ Drop **e** before adding ing

*	shear	shoe	shoot	shore
	sheer	shoo	chute	sure

shu shy si

shrine	s
shrink	ing, able, age, s
shrivel	led, ling, s
shrub	s
shrubber y	ies
shrug	ged, ging, s
shrunk	en
shudder	ed, ing, s
shuffle	d, ǿing, r, s
shun	ned, ning, s
shunt	ed, ing, er, s
shut	ting, s
shutter	ed, ing, s
shuttle	d, ǿing, cock, s
shy	er, est, ly, ness

si

sick	er, est, ly, ness, -bay, -bed, -room
sicken	ed, ing, s
side	d, ǿing, car, light, line, -show, s
sideboard	s
sideways	
siege	s
sieve	d, ǿing, s
sift	ed, ing, er, s
sigh	ed, ing, s
sight* (see)	ed, ing, less, seeing, seer, s
sign	ed, ing, board, -writer, post, s
signal	led, ling, ler, man, men, s
signal-box	es
signature	-tune, s
signet* (a seal)	-ring, s
significance	
significant	ly
signify	ing
signif ied	ies

silence	d, ǿing, r, s
silent	ly
silhouette	d, ǿing, s
silk	en, worm, s
silk y	ier, iest, ily, iness
sill y	ier, iest, ily, iness, ies
silver	ed, ing, y, -paper, -plated
similar	ly
similarit y	ies
simmer	ed, ing, s
simple	r, st, ness, ton, -minded
simplicity	
simply	
simplify	ing
simplif ied	ication, ies
simultaneous	ly, ness
sin	ned, ning, ner, s
since	
sincere	r, st, ly, ness
sincerity	
sing	ing, er, -song, s
singe	d, ing, s
single	d, ǿing, ǿy, -handed, s
singular	ly, s
sinister	ly
sink	ing, er, s
sip	ped, ping, per, s
siphon	ed, ing, s
sister	ly, s
sister(s)-**in-law**	
sit	ting, ter, s
sitting-room	s
site* (a place)	d, ǿing, s
situated	
situation	s
size	d, ǿing, s
sizzle	d, ǿing, s

ǿ Drop **e** before adding *ing*

*	sight	signet
	site	cygnet

sk sl

sk

skate	d, ∮ing, r, board, s
skating-rink	s
skein	s
skeleton	s
sketch	ed, ing, es
sketch y	ier, iest, ily, iness
skewer	ed, ing, s
ski	-ed, -ing, er, -jump, -lift, -run, s
skid	ded, ding, s
skilful	ly, ness
skill	ed, s
skim	med, ming, mer, s
skin	ned, ning, -diving, -diver, s
skinn y	ier, iest, iness
skip	ped, ping, per, s
skipping-rope	s
skipper	ed, ing, s
skirmish	ed, ing, es
skirt	ed, ing, s
skittle	d, ∮ing, r, -alley, -ball, -pin, s
skull* (head bones)	-cap, s
skulk	ed, ing, s
skunk	s
sky	ing, lark, light, -rocket, scraper
sk ied	ies

sl

slack	ed, ing, er, est, ly, ness, s
slacken	ed, ing, s
slain	
slam	med, ming, s
slang	ing, y
slant	ed, ing, wise, s
slap	ped, ping, per, dash, stick, s
slash	ed, ing, es

slate	s
slaughter	ed, ing, er, -house, s
slave	d, ∮ing, r, ry, -driver, -trader, s
slay* (kill)	ing, er, s
sledge	d, ∮ing, r, s
sleek	ed, ing, er, est, ly, ness, s
sleep	ing, er, less, -walking, -walker, s
sleep y	ier, iest, ily, iness
slept	
sleet	ed, ing, s
sleet y	ier, iest, iness
sleeve	d, less, -button, s
sleigh* (sledge)	ing, -bell, -horse, s
slender	ly, ness
sleuth	-hound, s
slew	
slice	d, ∮ing, r, s
slick	ed, ing, er, est, ly, ness, s
slid	
slide	∮ing, r, s
slight	ed, ing, er, est, ly, ness, s
slim	med, ming, mer, mest, ly, ness, s
slime	
slim y	ier, iest, ily, iness
sling	ing, er, s
slink	ing, er, s
slink y	ier, iest, ily, iness
slip	ped, ping, knot, shod, way, s
slipper	s
slipper y	ier, iest, ily, iness
slit	ting, ter, s
slither	ed, ing, y, s
sloe* (wild plum)	-tree, s
slog	ged, ging, ger, s
slogan	s
slop	ped, ping, -basin, s
slopp y	ier, iest, ily, iness

∮ Drop **e** before adding *ing*

*	skull		slay	sloe
	scull		sleigh	slow

sm

slope	d, ẹing, s
slot	ted, ting, -machine, -meter, s
slouch	ed, ing, es
slovenly	ier, iest, iness
slow*	ed, ing, er, est, ly, ness, s
slow-worm	s
slug	s
sluggish	ly, ness
sluice	d, ẹing, -gate, s
slum	my, -dweller, s
slumber	ed, ing, er, s
slump	ed, ing, s
slung	
slunk	
slush	ed, ing, es
slushy	ier, iest, ily, iness
sly	er, est, ly, ness

sm

smack	ed, ing, s
small	er, est, ness
smart	ed, ing, er, est, ly, ness, s
smarten	ed, ing, s
smash	ed, ing, es
smear	ed, ing, s
smeary	ier, iest, ily, iness
smell	ed, ing, er, s
smelly	ier, iest, ily, iness
smelt or **smelled**	
smile	d, ẹing, r, s
smirk	ed, ing, er, s
smithereens	
smock	ed, ing, s
smoke	d, ẹing, r, -bomb, -screen, s
smoky	ier, iest, ily, iness
smooth	ed, ing, er, est, ly, ness, s

sn

smother	ed, ing, s
smoulder	ed, ing, s
smudge	d, ẹing, s
smudgy	ier, iest, ily, iness
smuggle	d, ẹing, r, s
smut	ted, ting, s
smutty	ier, iest, ily, iness

sn

snack	-bar, s
snail	s
snake	d, ẹing, ẹy, -bite, -charmer, s
snap	ped, ping, per, shot, dragon, s
snare	d, ẹing, r, s
snarl	ed, ing, er, s
snatch	ed, ing, es
sneak	ed, ing, er, s
sneaky	ier, iest, ily, iness
sneer	ed, ing, er, s
sneeze	d, ẹing, r, s
sniff	ed, ing, er, s
sniffle	d, ẹing, r, s
snigger	ed, ing, er, s
snip	ped, ping, per, s
snipe	d, ẹing, r, s
snivel	led, ling, ler, s
snob	bery, bish, bishness, s
snooker	ed
snore	d, ẹing, r, s
snort	ed, ing, er, s
snow	ed, ing, drift, fall, flake, storm, s
snow	man, men, -plough, drop, shoe, s
snowball	ed, ing, s
snowy	ier, iest, ily, iness
snug	ger, gest, ly, ness
snuggle	d, ẹing, s

ẹ Drop **e** before adding *ing*

* slow
  sloe

so

soak *ed, ing, s*
soap *ed, ing, -suds, -bubble, -flake, s*
soap*y* *ier, iest, ily, iness*
soar* (fly upwards) *ed, ing, s*
sob *bed, bing, s*
sociable *ness*
social *ly, s*
socialist *s*
societ*y* *ies*
sock *s*
socket *s*
soda *-bread, -fountain, -water*
sodden
sofa *s*
soft *er, est, ish, ly, ness, -hearted*
soften *ed, ing, er, s*
sogg*y* *ier, iest, ily, iness*
soil *ed, ing, s*
sold* (sell)
solder *ed, ing, s*
soldier *ed, ing, s*
sole* (only) *ly*
sole* (bottom-of shoe, etc.) *d,* ɇ*ing, s*
sole* (fish) *s* or **sole**
solemn *ity, ly, ness*
solicitor *s*
solid *ity, ly, s*
solitary
solo *ist, -singer, s*
solution *s*
solve *d, ɇing, s*
some* *body, one, how, thing, where*
sometime *s*
somersault *ed, ing, s*
son* (boy) *ny, s*
song *ster, -book, -bird, -writer, s*
soon *er, est*
soot
soot*y* *ier, iest, ily, iness*
soothe *d, ɇing, s*
soprano *s*
sore* (painful) *r, st, ly, ness, s*
sorrow *ed, ing, ful, fully, s*
sorr*y* *ier, iest, ily, iness*
sort *ed, ing, er, s*
soul* (spirit) *ful, fully, s*
sound *ed, ing, er, est, ly, ness, s*
soup *-plate, -spoon, s*
sour *ed, ing, er, est, ly, ness, s*
source *s*
south *-east, -west, ern, erly, ward*
souvenir *s*
sovereign *s*
sow* (scatter seed) *ed, ing, er, s*
sown* (planted)

sp

space *d, ɇing, r, s, craft, man, men*
space *-capsule, ship, -station, suit, s*
spacious *ly, ness*
spade *ful, s*
spaghetti
span *ned, ning, s*
spangle *d, ɇing, s*
spaniel *s*
spank *ed, ing, s*
spanner *s*
spare *d, ɇing, s*
spark *ed, ing, s*
sparkle *d, ɇing, r, s*
sparrow *-hawk, s*
spastic *s*

ɇ Drop **e** before adding *ing*

*						
soar	sold	sole	some	son	sow	sown
sore	soled	soul	sum	sun	sew	sewn
					so	

spe   sph   spi   spl   spo   spr   spu   spy

spat	
spawn	*ed, ing, s*
speak	*ing, er, s*
spear	*ed, ing, man, men, head, -gun, s*
special	*ly, ty, ist, ity*
specialize	*d, ɇing, s*
specimen	*s*
speck	*ed, ing, less, lessly, s*
speckle	*d, ɇing, s*
spectacle	*s*
spectacular	*ly*
spectator	*s*
spectre	*s*
sped or **speeded**	
speech	*-training, less, es*
speed	*ed, ing, -boat, -limit, way, s*
speed *y*	*ier, iest, ily, iness*
spell	*ed, ing, er, bind, bound, s*
spelt or **spelled**	
spend	*ing, er, thrift, s*
spent	
sphere	*s*
spider	*y, s*
spied	
spike	*d, ɇing, s*
spill	*ed, ing, s*
spilt or **spilled**	
spin	*ning, ner, -dryer, s*
spinach	
spinster	*s*
spiral	*led, ling, ly, s*
spire	*s*
spirit	*ed, ing, -level, -lamp, s*
spirt or **spurt**	*ed, ing, s*
spit	*ting, ter, s*
spite	*d, ɇing, s*
spiteful	*ly, ness*

splash	*ed, ing, es*
splendid	*ly*
splendour	*s*
splint	*s*
splinter	*ed, ing, y, s*
split	*ting, ter, s*
splutter	*ed, ing, er, s*
spoil	*ed, ing, er, -sport, s*
spoilt or **spoiled**	
spoke (speak)	*n, sman, smen*
spoke (of wheel)	*s*
sponge	*d, ɇing, r, -bag, -cake, s*
spong *y*	*ier, iest, ily, iness*
spool	*s*
spoon	*ed, ing, ful, s*
sport	*ed, ing, sman, smen, s*
sport *y*	*ier, iest, ily, iness*
spot	*ted, ting, ter, less, lessly, light, s*
spott *y*	*ier, iest, ily, iness*
spout	*ed, ing, s*
sprain	*ed, ing, s*
sprang	
sprat	*s* or **sprat**
sprawl	*ed, ing, er, s*
spray	*ed, ing, er, s*
spread	*ing, er, s*
spring	*ing, -cleaning, -board, time, s*
spring *y*	*ier, iest, ily, iness*
sprinkle	*d, ɇing, r, s*
sprint	*ed, ing, er, s*
sprout	*ed, ing, s*
sprung	
spun	
spur	*red, ring, s*
spurt or **spirt**	*ed, ing, s*
spy	*ing*
sp *ied*	*ies*

*ɇ Drop **e** before adding ing*

88

sq st_a   ste

sq

squabble	d, ∉ing, r, s
squad	ron, s
squall	ed, ing, y, s
squander	ed, ing, er, s
square	d, ∉ing, ly, ness, -dance, root, s
squash	ed, ing, y, es
squat	ted, ting, ter, s
squaw	s
squawk	ed, ing, er, s
squeak	ed, ing, er, s
squeak y	ier, iest, ily, iness
squeal	ed, ing, er, s
squeeze	d, ∉ing, r, s
squelch	ed, ing, es
squib	s
squint	ed, ing, er, s
squire	d, ∉ing, s
squirm	ed, ing, er, s
squirrel	s
squirt	ed, ing, er, s

st

stab	bed, bing, ber, s
stable	d, ∉ing, -man, -men, -boy, s
stack	ed, ing, s
stadium	s or **stadia**
staff	ed, ing, -room, s
stag	-beetle, -horn, hound, -hunt, s
stage	d, ∉ing, -hand, -manager, s
stage-coach	es
stagger	ed, ing, er, s
stain	ed, ing, less, er, s
stair*	-carpet, case, -rod, way, s
stake* (a stick; bet)	d, ∉ing, s
stale	r, st, ly, ness

stalk	ed, ing, er, s
stall	ed, ing, -holder, s
stallion	s
stammer	ed, ing, er, s
stamp	ed, ing, -album, -collector, s
stampede	d, ∉ing, s
stand	ing, s
standard	-bearer, s
star	red, ring, less, light, lit, s
starr y	ier, iest, ily, iness
starboard	
starfish	es or **starfish**
starch	ed, ing, es
stare* (look at)	d, ∉ing, s
starling	s
start	ed, ing, er, s
startle	d, ∉ing, s
starvation	
starve	d, ∉ing, s
state	d, ∉ing, ment, s
statel y	ier, iest, ily, iness
station	ed, ing, -master, s
stationary* (still)	
stationer	s
stationery* (paper, pens, etc.)	
statue	tte, s
staunch	ed, ing, er, est, ly, ness, es
stay	ed, ing, er, s
steady	ing
stead ied	ier, iest, ily, iness, ies
steak* (meat)	s
steal* (thieve)	ing, s
stealth	
stealth y	ier, iest, ily, iness
steam	ed, ing, er, boat, ship, -engine, s
steam y	ier, iest, ily, iness
steel* (metal)	ed, ing, y, work, worker, s

∉ Drop **e** before adding *ing*

*				
	stair	stake	stationary	steal
	stare	steak	stationery	steel

steep	er, est, ly, ness	**stool**	-ball, s
steeple	chase, jack, s	**stoop**	ed, ing, s
steer	age, ed, ing, er, sman, smen, s	**stop**	ped, ping, page, per, s
steering-wheel	s	**storage**	
stem	med, ming, s	**store**	d, ∅ing, house, keeper, -room, s
stencil	led, ling, ler, s	**storey*** (floor)	s
step	ped, ping, -ladder, s	**stork**	s
step	father, mother, brother, sister, s	**storm**	ed, ing, -cloud, s
stepping-stone	s	**storm** y	ier, iest, ily, iness
sterilize	d, ∅ing, r, s	**stor** y* (tale; floor)	ies
stern	er, est, ly, ness	**stout**	er, est, ly, ness, ish, hearted
stew	ed, ing, er, -pot, s	**stove**	-pipe, s
steward	s	**stow**	ed, ing, away, s
stewardess	es	**straggle**	d, ∅ing, r, s
stick	ing, er, -insect, s	**straight*** (not bent)	er, est, ly, ness
stick y	ier, iest, ily, iness	**straighten**	ed, ing, er, s
stickleback	s	**strain**	ed, ing, er, s
stiff	er, est, ly, ness	**strait*** (sea channel)	s
stiffen	ed, ing, er, s	**strand**	ed, ing, s
stifle	d, ∅ing, r, s	**strange**	r, st, ly, ness
stile* (steps)	s	**stranger**	s
still	ed, ing, ness, s	**strangle**	d, ∅ing, hold, r, s
sting	ing, er, s	**strap**	ped, ping, less, s
stinging-nettle	s	**straw**	board, -coloured, -hat, s
stir	red, ring, rer, s	**strawberr** y	ies
stirrup	s	**stray**	ed, ing, er, s
stitch	ed, ing, es	**streak**	ed, ing, er, s
stoat	s	**streak** y	ier, iest, ily, iness
stock	ed, ing, ist, -car, -pot, -room, s	**stream**	ed, ing, lined, er, s
stocking	s	**street**	-sweeper, s
stockade	d, ∅ing, s	**strength**	s
stoke	d, ∅ing, r, s	**strengthen**	ed, ing, er, s
stole	n	**strenuous**	ly, ness
stomach	-ache, -pump, s	**stretch**	ed, ing, es
stone	d, ∅ing, -cold, -deaf, -mason, s	**stretcher**	-bearer, s
ston y	ier, iest, ily, iness	**strict**	er, est, ly, ness
stood		**stride**	∅ing, r, s

∅ Drop **e** before adding *ing*

*   stile   storey   straight
     style   story   strait

strike	*ǿing, r, s*
string	*ing, -bag, -vest, s*
strip	*ped, ping, per, -lighting, s*
stripe	*d, ǿing, s*
strode	
stroke	*d, ǿing, r, s*
stroll	*ed, ing, er, s*
strong	*er, est, ly, ish, hold, -room*
struck	
structure	*s*
struggle	*d, ǿing, r, s*
strum	*med, ming, mer, s*
strung	
strut	*ted, ting, ter, s*
stub	*bed, bing, by, s*
stubborn	*ly, ness*
stuck	
stud	*ded, ding, s*
student	*s*
studio	*s*
studious	*ly, ness*
study	*ing*
stud *ied*	*ies*
stuff	*ed, ing, er, s*
stuff *y*	*ier, iest, ily, iness*
stumble	*d, ǿing, r, s*
stump	*ed, ing, s*
stump *y*	*ier, iest, ily, iness*
stun	*ned, ning, ner, s*
stung	
stunt	*ed, ing, man, men, s*
stupendous	*ly, ness*
stupid	*ity, ly*
sturd *y*	*ier, iest, ily, iness*
stutter	*ed, ing, er, s*
st *y*	*ies*
style* (way; fashion)	*d, ǿing, s*

	su
subject	*ed, ing, s*
submarine	*r, s*
submerge	*d, ǿing, s*
submit	*ted, ting, s*
subscribe	*d, ǿing, r, s*
subscription	*s*
subside	*d, ǿing, s*
substance	*s*
substantial	*ly*
substitute	*d, ǿing, s*
subtract	*ed, ing, ion, s*
suburb	*s*
succeed	*ed, ing, s*
success	*es*
successful	*ly*
succession	*s*
successor	*s*
such	*like*
suck	*ed, ing, er, s*
suction	*-pump*
sudden	*ly, ness*
suds	
suet	*-pudding, y*
suffer	*ed, ing, er, s*
sufficient	*ly*
suffocate	*d, ǿing, s*
suffocation	
sugar	*ed, ing, y, -basin, -beet, -cane, s*
suggest	*ed, ing, ion, s*
suicide	*s*
suit	*ed, ing, able, ably, ability, case, s*
suite* (set of furniture, rooms, etc.)	*s*
sulk	*ed, ing, s*
sulk *y*	*ier, iest, ily, iness*
sullen	*ly, ness*
sultana	*s*

ǿ Drop **e** before adding *ing*

*** style	suite
stile	sweet

sum* (add up; total)	*med, ming, s*
summer	*y, -time, -house, s*
summit	*s*
summon	*ed, ing, s*
summons	*es*
sumptuous	*ly, ness*
sun*	*ned, ning, beam, light, flower, s*
sun*	*-glasses, rise, set, shine, shade, s*
sunn *y*	*ier, iest, ily, iness*
sunbathe	*d, ɇing, r, s*
sunburn	*ed, t*
sundae* (ice cream)	*⚡ s*
Sunday*	*-school, s*
sung	
sunk	*en*
superb	*ly*
superintend	*ed, ing, ent, s*
superior	*ity, s*
supermarket	*s*
superstition	*s*
superstitious	*ly, ness*
supervise	*d, ɇing, s*
supervision	
supervisor	*s*
supper	*-time, s*
supple	*ness*
supply	*ing*
suppl *ied*	*ier, ies*
support	*ed, ing, er, s*
suppose	*d, ɇing, s*
sure* (certain)	*r, st, ly, ness, -footed*
surf* (sea foam)	*ing, -board, -riding*
surface	*d, ɇing, s*
surge	*d, ɇing, s*
surgeon	*s*
surger *y*	*ies*
surname	*s*

surplice* (gown)	*s*
surplus* (left over)	*es*
surprise	*d, ɇing, s*
surrender	*ed, ing, s*
surround	*ed, ing, s*
survey	*ed, ing, or, s*
survival	
survive	*d, ɇing, s*
survivor	*s*
suspect	*ed, ing, s*
suspend	*ed, ing, er, s*
suspense	
suspicion	*s*
suspicious	*ly, ness*
sustain	*ed, ing, s*

SW

swagger	*ed, ing, er, -cane, -coat, -stick, s*
swallow	*ed, ing, er, s*
swam	
swamp	*ed, ing, s*
swamp *y*	*ier, iest, ily, iness*
swan	*s*
swap or **swop**	*ped, ping, per, s*
swarm	*ed, ing, s*
swarth *y*	*ier, iest, ily, iness*
sway	*ed, ing, s*
swear	*ing, er, -word, s*
sweat	*ed, ing, y, er, -band, -shirt, -suit, s*
swede	*s*
sweep	*ing, er, stake, s*
swept	
sweet*	*er, est, ish, ly, ness, heart, -pea, s*
sweeten	*ed, ing, er, s*
swell	*ed, ing, s*
swelter	*ed, ing, s*

*ɇ Drop **e** before adding ing*

*	sum	sun	sundae	sure	surf	surplice	sweet
	some	son	Sunday	shore	serf	surplus	suite

sy   ta

swept	
swerve	d, ęing, s
swift	er, est, ly, ness, s
swill	ed, ing, s
swim	mer, suit, s
swimming	-bath, -pool
swindle	d, ęing, r, s
swine	herd. **swine**
swing	ing, er, s
swipe	d, ęing, r, s
swirl	ed, ing, s
swish	ed, ing, es
switch	ed, ing, es
swivel	led, ling, s
swollen	
swoon	ed, ing, s
swoop	ed, ing, s
swop or **swap**	ped, ping, per, s
sword	sman, smen, -dance, s
swordfish	es or **swordfish**
swore	
sworn	
swum	
swung	

sy

sycamore	-tree, s
sympathetic	ally
sympathize	d, ęing, r, s
sympath y	ies
symphon y	ies
symptom	s
synagogue	s
syringe	d, ęing, s
syrup	y
system	atic, atically, s

ta

tabby-cat	s
table	-tennis, -cloth, -mat, s
table-spoon	ful, s
tableau	x or s
tablet	s
tack	ed, ing, s
tackle	d, ęing, r, s
tact	ful, fully, less, lessly
tactics	
tadpole	s
tag	ged, ging, s
tail*	ed, ing, -end, -lamp, -light, -spin, s
tailor	ed, ing, -made, s
take	n, ęing, r, -away, -off, s
talcum powder	
tale* (story)	-bearer, -teller, s
talent	ed, s
talk	ative, ed, ing, er, s
tall	er, est, ish, ness
tambourine	s
tame	d, ęing, r, st, ly, ness, s
tamper	ed, ing, er, s
tan	ned, ning, ner, s
tandem	s
tangerine	s
tangle	d, ęing, s
tango	ed, ing, s
tank	er, ful, -trap, s
tankard	s
tantalize	d, ęing, s
tantrum	s
tap	ped, ping, per, -dance, -dancing, s
tape	d, ęing, s
tape	-measure, -recorder, -recording, s
tapestr y	ies
tapioca	

ę Drop **e** before adding *ing*

* tail / tale

te

tar	red, ring, ry, s
tarantula	s
tare* (weed)	s
target	s
tarnish	ed, ing, es
tarpaulin	s
tart	let, s
tartan	s
task	ed, ing, master, s
tassel	s
taste	d, ∉ing, r, s
tasteful	ly, ness
tasteless	ly, ness
tatter	ed, ing, s
tattoo	ed, ing, er, ist, -mark, s
taught* (teach)	
taunt	ed, ing, er, s
taut* (tight)	er, est, ly, ness
tavern	s
tax	ation, ed, ing, es
taxi	-cab, -driver, -rank, s

te

tea*	cake, -cloth, cup, pot, -service, s
tea*	-set, -things, -time, -table, -tray, s
tea-cos y	ies
tea-leaf	-leaves
tea-part y	ies
tea-spoon	ful, s
teach	ing, ings, es
teacher	s
teak	
team* (side; number)	-work, s
tear* (pull apart)	ing, s
tear	-gas, -drop, s
tearful	ly, ness

tease	d, ∉ing, r, s
technical	ly
technician	s
Teddy bear	s
tedious	ly, ness
tee* (golf)	d, ing, -shot, s
tee-shirt or **T-shirt**	s
teem* (pour; swarm)	ed, ing, s
teenage	d, -boy, -girl
teenager	s
teeth	
telegram	s
telegraph	ed, ing, -line, -pole, -wire, s
telephone	d, ∉ing, s
telescope	d, ∉ing, s
televise	d, ∉ing, s
television	s
tell	ing, er, -tale, s
temper	ed, ing, s
temperature	s
temple	s
temporar y	ily
tempt	ation, ed, ing, er, s
tend	ed, ing, s
tender	-hearted, ly, ness
tenement	s
tennis	-ball, -court, -racket
tenor	s
tense	d, ∉ing, r, st, ly, ness, s
tent	-peg, -pole, -rope, s
tentacle	s
tepid	ly, ness
term	ly, ed, ing, s
terminus	es or **termini**
terrace	d, ∉ing, -house, s
terrible	ness
terribly	

∉ Drop **e** before adding *ing*

★	tare	taught		tea	team
	tear	taut		tee	teem

th

terrier	s	thermometer	s
terrific	ally	thermos flask	s
terrify	ing	these	
terrif ied	ies	they	
territorial	s	they'll (they will; they shall)	
territor y	ies	they're* (they are)	
terror	ism, ist, -stricken, s	they've (they have)	
terrorize	d, ǿing, s	thick	er, est, ly, ness, ish, -skinned
test	ed, ing, -paper, -piece, -tube, s	thicken	ed, ing, er, s
testament	s	thicket	s
testimonial	s	thief	thieves
tetanus		thieve	d, ǿing, s
tether	ed, ing, s	thimble	ful, s
text	-book, s	thin	ned, ning, ner, nest, ly, ness, s
textile	s	thing	s
		think	ing, er, s
		thirst	ed, ing, s
		thirst y	ier, iest, ily, iness

th

than		this	
thank	ed, ing, -offering, s	thistle	s
thankful	ly, ness	thorn	s
thankless	ly, ness	thorn y	ier, iest, ily, iness
that		thorough	ly, ness, bred, fare
that's (that is)		those	
thatch	ed, ing, es	though	
thaw	ed, ing, s	thought	-reader, s
theatre	-ticket, s	thoughtful	ly, ness
theatrical	ly, s	thoughtless	ly, ness
theft	s	thrash	ed, ing, ings, es
their* (belonging to them)		thread	ed, ing, bare, er, s
theirs* (belonging to them)		threat	s
them	selves	threaten	ed, ing, s
then		thresh	ed, ing, es
theor y	ies	threw* (throw)	
there* (in that place)	abouts, after	thrift	less
therefore		thrift y	ier, iest, ily, iness
there's* (there is)		thrill	ed, ing, er, s

ǿ Drop **e** before adding *ing*

	their	theirs		threw
*	there	there's		through
	they're			

ti   to

thrive	*d, ǿing, s*
throat	*s*
throb	*bed, bing, s*
throne* (king's seat)	*s*
throng	*ed, ing, s*
throttle	*d, ǿing, s*
through* (from end to end)	*out*
throw	*ing, er, n,* s*
thrush	*es*
thrust	*ing, s*
thud	*ded, ding, s*
thug	*s*
thumb	*ed, ing, -mark, -nail, screw, s*
thump	*ed, ing, er, s*
thunder	*ed, ing, y, bolt, clap, storm, s*
Thursday	*s*

ti

tiara	*s*
tick	*ed, ing, s*
ticket	*-collector, -office, s*
tickle	*d, ǿing, r, s*
ticklish	*ly, ness*
tide* (sea)	*-mark, s*
tidings	
tidy	*ing*
tidied	*ier, iest, ily, iness, ies*
tie	*d,* -clip, -pin, s*
tying	
tiger	*-cat, -moth, s*
tigress	*es*
tight er, est, ly, ness, -rope, s
tighten	*ed, ing, er, s*
tile	*d, ǿing, r, s*
till	*ed, ing, er, s*
till or **until**	

tilt	*ed, ing, er, s*
timber	*ed, -mill, -yard, s*
time	*d, ǿing, r, ly, less, -bomb, table, s*
timid	*ity, ly, ness*
tin	*ned, ning, ny, -opener, foil, -tack, s*
tinge	*d, ǿing, s*
tingle	*d, ǿing, s*
tinker	*ed, ing, s*
tinkle	*d, ǿing, s*
tinsel	*led, ling, ly*
tint	*ed, ing, s*
tiny	*ier, iest, ily, iness*
tip	*ped, ping, per, ster, s*
tiptoe	*d, ing, s*
tire* (weary)	*d, ǿing, some, s*
tired	*ness*
tireless	*ly, ness*
tissue	*-paper, s*
title	*d, s*
titter	*ed, ing, s*

to

to* (towards)	
toad	*-in-the-hole, s*
toadstool	*s*
to and fro	
toast	*ed, ing, er, -rack, s*
tobacco	*nist, -pipe, -plant, s*
toboggan	*ed, ing, er, s*
today or **to-day**	
toddle	*d, ǿing, r, s*
toe*	*d, ing, -cap, -hold, -nail, s*
toffee	*-apple, s*
together	*ness*
toil	*ed, ing, er, s*
toilet	*-paper, -roll, -soap, s*

ǿ Drop **e** before adding *ing*

*	throne	through	tide		tire	toe	to
	thrown	threw	tied		tyre	tow	too
							two (2)

token	*s*	**toss**	*ed, ing, es*
told		**total**	*led, ling, ly, s*
tolerate	*d, øing, s*	**totter**	*ed, ing, y, er, s*
toll	*ed, ing, -bridge, -gate, s*	**touch**	*ed, ing, y, es*
tomahawk	*s*	**tough**	*er, est, ly, ness, s*
tomato	*es*	**toughen**	*ed, ing, s*
tomb	*stone, s*	**tour**	*ed, ing, ist, s*
tomcat	*s*	**tournament**	*s*
tomorrow or **to-morrow**	*s*	**tousle**	*d, øing, s*
tomtit	*s*	**tow*** (pull)	*ed, ing, -line, -path, -rope, s*
ton or **tonne** (metric)	*s*	**towards** or **toward**	
tone	*d, øing, -deaf, s*	**towel**	*led, ling, -rail, s*
tongs		**tower**	*ed, ing, -block, s*
tongue	*-tied, -twister, s*	**town**	*-council, -crier, -hall, s*
tonic	*s*	**toy**	*ed, ing, shop, s*
tonight or **to-night**			
tonsil	*s*		
tonsillitis			

too* (more than enough; also)

took

tool *-bag, -chest, -shed, s*

tooth *ache, paste, powder, less,* **teeth**

tooth-brush *es*

top *ped, ping, per, knot, -heavy, -hat, s*

topic *s*

topple *d, øing, s*

topsy-turvy

torch *es*

tore

torment *ed, ing, or, s*

torn

tornado *es*

torpedo *ed, ing, es*

torrent *s*

torrential *ly*

tortoise *-shell, s*

torture *d, øing, r, -chamber, s*

tr

trace *d, øing, r, s*

tracing-paper

track *ed, ing, er, suit, s*

tractor *s*

trade *d, øing, mark, sman, smen, r, s*

traffic *-sign, -signal, -lights*

traged*y* *ies*

tragic *ally*

trail *ed, ing, er, s*

train *ed, ing, er, s*

traitor *ous, ously, s*

tramp *ed, ing, er, s*

trample *d, øing, r, s*

trampoline *s*

transfer *red, ring, able, s*

transform *ed, ing, ation, s*

transistor *-radio, s*

translate *d, øing, s*

translation *s*

ø Drop **e** before adding *ing*

*	too	tow
	to	toe
	two (2)	

transparent	ly, ness	**trim**	med, ming, mer, mest, ly, ness, s
transport ed, ing, er, ation, able, s		**trinket**	s
trap ped, ping, per, -door, s		**trio**	s
trapeze	s	**trip**	ped, ping, per, s
travel	led, ling, ler, s	**triple**	d, øing, s
trawl	ed, ing, er, s	**triplet**	s
tray	-cloth, ful, s	**tripod**	s
treacherous	ly, ness	**triumph**	ed, ing, ant, antly, s
treacher y	ies	**trod**	den
treacle		**trolley**	s
tread	ing, s	**trombone**	øist, s
treason	able	**troop*** (of scouts, soldiers)	ed, ing, er, s
treasure d, øing, r, -chest, -hunt, s		**troph** y	ies
treat	ed, ing, ment, s	**tropic**	al, ally, s
treble	d, øing, s	**trot**	ted, ting, ter, s
tree -stump, -top, -trunk, s		**trouble**	d, øing, some, -maker, s
trek	ked, king, ker, s	**trough**	s
trellis	-work	**troupe*** (of entertainers)	r, s
tremble	d, øing, s	**trousers**	
tremendous	ly, ness	**trousseau**	x or s
trench	es	**trout**	trout
trespass	ed, ing, es	**trowel**	s
trespasser	s	**truant**	s
trestle	-table, s	**truck**	-load, s
trial	s	**trudge**	d, øing, s
triangle	s	**true**	r, st, ness
tribe	sman, smen, s	**truly**	
tributar y	ies	**trumpet**	ed, ing, er, -call, s
trick	ed, ing, ery, ster, s	**truncheon**	s
trick y	ier, iest, ily, iness	**trunk**	s
trickle	d, øing, s	**truss**	ed, ing, es
tricycle	d, øing, s	**trust**	ed, ing, worthy, s
tried		**trust** y	ier, iest, ily, iness
trier	s	**truth**	s
tries		**truthful**	ly, ness
trifle	d, øing, s	**try**	ing
trigger	ed, ing, s	**tr** ied	ier, ies

ø Drop **e** before adding *ing*

tu   tw   ty   ug   um

tu

tuba	s
tubb y	ier, iest, iness
tube	ǿing, less, -train, s
tuck	ed, ing, -shop, s
Tudor	s
Tuesday	s
tuft	s
tug	ged, ging, ger, boat, s
tug-of-war	
tuition	
tulip	s
tumble	d, ǿing, r, down, -dryer, s
tumbler	ful, s
tumult	s
tumultuous	ly, ness
tundra	s
tune	d, ǿing, r, s
tuneful	ly, ness
tuneless	ly, ness
tunic	s
tunnel	led, ling, ler, s
turban	s
turbine	s
turf	ed, ing, s or **turves**
turkey	cock, s
Turkish delight	
turmoil	
turn	ed, ing, er, over, stile, table, s
turnip	s
turpentine	
turquoise	s
turret	ed, s
turtle	-neck, -shell, -soup, -dove, 's
tusk	s
tussle	d, ǿing, s
tutor	ial, s

tw

twang	ed, ing, s
tweed	s
tweezers	
twice	
twiddle	d, ǿing, r, s
twig	s
twilight	
twin	ned, ning, -brother, -sister, s
twine	d, ǿing, s
twinge	d, ǿing, s
twinkle	d, ǿing, s
twirl	ed, ing, s
twist	ed, ing, er, s
twist y	ier, iest, ily, iness
twitch	ed, ing, es
twitter	ed, ing, s

ty

tying	
type	d, ǿing, written, writing, writer, s
typist	s
typhoon	s
typical	ly, ness
tyrannize	d, ǿing, s
tyrant	s
tyre* (wheel cover)	s

ug

ugl y	ier, iest, ily, iness

um

umbrella	-stand, s
umpire	d, ǿing, s

ǿ Drop **e** before adding *ing*

* tyre
tire

un

un		**undertake**	n, ǿing, r, s
unable		**undertook**	
unafraid		**undid**	
unaided		**undo**	ing
unarm	ed, ing, s	**undone**	
unattractive	ly, ness	**undoubted**	ly
unavoidabl e	y	**undress**	ed, ing, es
unaware	s	**uneas** y	ier, iest, ily, iness
unbalance	d, ǿing, s	**unemploy** ed	ment
unbearabl e	y	**uneven**	ly, ness
unbeaten		**unexpected**	ly, ness
unbolt	ed, ing, s	**unexplored**	
unbuckle	d, ǿing, s	**unfair**	ly, ness
unbutton	ed, ing, s	**unfasten**	ed, ing, s
uncann y	ily, iness	**unfinished**	
uncertain	ly, ty	**unfit**	ted, ting, s
uncivilized		**unfold**	ed, ing, s
uncle	s	**unfortunate**	ly
unclean	liness	**unfriendl** y	iness
uncomfortable	ness	**unfurnished**	
uncommon	ly, ness	**ungrateful**	ly, ness
unconscious	ly, ness	**unguarded**	ly, ness
uncork	ed, ing, s	**unhapp** y	ier, iest, ily, iness
uncover	ed, ing, s	**unharmed**	
uncurl	ed, ing, s	**unhealth** y	ier, iest, ily, iness
undamaged		**unhurt**	
undecided	ly	**uniform**	ed, s
under clothes, clothing, wear		**unimportant**	
under go, going, goes, gone, went		**uninhabited**	
undercurrent	s	**uninjured**	
underground		**uninteresting**	
undergrowth		**Union Jack**	s
underneath		**unite**	d, ǿing, s
understand	able, ing, s	**universe**	
understood		**universit** y	ies
understudy	ing	**unjust**	ly, ness
understud ied	ies	**unkind**	er, est, ly, ness

ǿ Drop **e** before adding *ing*

unknown	
unlawful	ly, ness
unless	
unlike	ness
unlikel y	ier, iest, ihood
unload	ed, ing, s
unlock	ed, ing, s
unluck y	ier, iest, ily, iness
unmistakabl e	y
unnecessar y	ily
unoccupied	
unpack	ed, ing, s
unpleasant	ly, ness
unpopular	ity, ly
unravel	led, ling, s
unreasonabl e	y
unreliable	ness
unroll	ed, ing, s
unsaddle	d, ǿing, s
unsafe	r, st, ly, ness
unscrew	ed, ing, s
unselfish	ly, ness
unstead y	ier, iest, ily, iness
unsuitable	
untangle	d, ǿing, s
untid y	ier, iest, ily, iness
untie	d, s
untying	
until or till	
untrue	
unusual	ly, ness
unveil	ed, ing, s
unwelcome	
unwell	
unwilling	ly, ness
unwise	ly
unwrap	ped, ping, s

up

upbringing	
upheaval	s
upholster	ed, ing, er, s
upholster y	ies
upkeep	
upon	
upper	most, -cut, s
upright	ly, ness, s
uprising	s
uproar	s
uproot	ed, ing, s
upset	ting, s
upside-down	
upstairs	
upstream	
upturn	ed, ing, s
upward	ly, s

ur

uranium	
urban	
urchin	s
urge	d, ǿing, s
urgenc y	ies
urgent	ly
urn* (vase; tea-urn)	s

us

use	d, ǿing, r, s
useful	ly, ness
useless	ly, ness
usher	ed, ing, s
usherette	s
usual	ly, ness

ǿ Drop **e** before adding *ing*

* urn
earn

ut	
utensil	s
utmost	
utter	ed, ing, ance, s
utter	ly, most, ness

va	
vacanc y	ies
vacant	ly
vacate	d, ǿing, s
vacation	s
vaccinate	d, ǿing, s
vacuum	-cleaner, -flask, s
vague	r, st, ly, ness
vain* (proud)	er, est, ly
vale* (valley)	s
valentine	s
valiant	ly
valley	s
valuable	s
value	d, ǿing, less, r, s
valve	s
vane* (weathercock)	s
vanilla	
vanish	ed, ing, es
vanit y	ies
vanquish	ed, ing, es
variet y	ies
various	ly, ness
varnish	ed, ing, es
vary	ing
var ied	ies
vase	s
vaseline	
vast	er, est, ly, ness
vault	ed, ing, er, s

ve	
veal	
vegetable	s
vegetarian	s
vegetation	
vehicle	s
veil* (a covering)	ed, ing, s
vein* (blood-vessel)	ed, ing, s
velvet	y, s
vengeance	
venison	
vent	ed, ing, -hole, s
ventilate	d, ǿing, s
ventilation	
ventilator	s
ventriloquist	s
venture	d, ǿing, some, s
veranda(h)	s
verb	al, ally, s
verdict	s
verge	d, ǿing, s
verger	s
vermilion	s
vermin	ous, ously
verse	s
version	s
versus	
vertical	ly
very	
vessel	s
vest	s
vestibule	s
vestr y	ies
vet	ted, ting, s
veteran	s
veterinar y	ies
vex	ed, ing, es, ation, atious

ǿ Drop **e** before adding *ing*

*	vain	vale
	vane	veil
	vein	

vi　　vo　vu　wa

vi

viaduct	s
vibrate	d, ∉ing, s
vibration	s
vicar	age, s
vice	-admiral, -captain, s
vicious	ly, ness
victim	s
victor	s
victorious	ly, ness
victor y	ies
victual	led, ling, ler, s
videotape	d, ∉ing, s
view	ed, ing, er, point, s
vigorous	ly, ness
vigour	
viking	s
vile	r, st, ly, ness
villa	s
village	r, s
villain* (scoundrel)	ous, ously, s
villein* (serf)	s
vine	yard, s
vinegar	y
violence	
violent	ly
violet	s
violin	ist, s
virtue	s
visibl e	y
visibility	
vision	s
visit	ed, ing, or, s
vital	ity, ly
vivarium	s or **vivaria**
vivid	ly, ness
vixen	s

vo

vocabular y	ies
vocalist	s
voice	d, ∉ing, s
volcano	es
vole	s
volley	ēd, ing, -ball, s
volt	age, s
volume	s
voluntar y	ily
volunteer	ed, ing, s
vomit	ed, ing, s
vote	d, ∉ing, r, s
vouch	ed, ing, es
voucher	s
vow	ed, ing, s
vowel	s
voyage	d, ∉ing, r, s

vu

vulgar	ity, ly
vulnerable	ness
vulture	s

wa

waddle	d, ∉ing, r, s
wade	d, ∉ing, r, s
wafer	s
waft	ed, ing, er, s
wag	ged, ging, ger, s
wage	d, ∉ing, r, -earner, s
waggle	d, ∉ing, r, s
wagon or **waggon**	er, -load, s
waif	s
wail	ed, ing, er, s

∉ Drop **e** before adding *ing*

*　villain
　villein

waist* (of body)	coat, s
wait* (stay; serve)	ed, ing, s
waiter	s
waitress	es
waiting-room	s
wake	d, ẹing, r, s
waken	ed, ing, er, s
walk	ed, ing, er, s
walking-stick	s
wall	ed, ing, chart, flower, paper, s
wallet	s
wallow	ed, ing, er, s
walnut	-tree, s
walrus	es
waltz	ed, ing, es
wand	s
wander	ed, ing, er, s
wangle	d, ẹing, r, s
want	ed, ing, s
war*	-dance, -paint, -path, ship, s
war-cry	ies
warrior	s
warble	d, ẹing, r, s
ward	ed, ing, en, er, s
wardrobe	s
ware* (goods)	house, s
warm	th, ed, ing, er, est, ish, ly, s
warn* (be careful)	ed, ing, er, s
warp	ed, ing, s
warrant	ed, ing, s
warren	s
wart	s
wary	ier, iest, ily, iness
wash	able, ed, ing, es
washer	s
wasn't (was not)	
wasp	s

waste*	d, ẹing, land, -bin, -paper, -pipe, s
wasteful	ly, ness
watch	ed, ing, man, men, es
watchful	ly, ness
water	ed, ing, -colour, cress, fall, proof, s
water-lily	ies
watery	ier, iest, ily, iness
wave	d, ẹing, s
waver	ed, ing, er, s
wavy	ier, iest, ily, iness
wax	ed, ing, en, es, works
waxy	ier, iest, ily, iness
way* (direction; manner; road)	lay, side, s

we

weak* (not strong)	er, est, ly, ness, -kneed
weaken	ed, ing, s
weakling	s
wealth	
wealthy	ier, iest, ily, iness
weapon	s
wear* (dressed in)	ing, er, s
weary	ing
wearied	ier, iest, ily, iness, ies
weasel	s
weather*	ed, ing, cock, -forecast, -vane, s
weave	d, ẹing, r, s
we'd (we had; we should; we would)	
wed	ded, ding, s
wedding	-cake, -card, -day, -ring, -bell, s
wedding-dress	es
wedge	d, ẹing, s
Wednesday	s
weed	ed, ing, er, -killer, s
weedy	ier, iest, iness
week* (seven days)	-day, -end, s

ẹ Drop **e** before adding ing

waist	wait	war	ware	warn	way	weak	weather
waste	weight	wore	wear	worn	weigh	week	whether

wh

weekly — ies	**where** *abouts, as, by, fore, upon*
weep *ing, y, er, s*	**wherever**
wept	**whether*** (if)
weigh* (measure heaviness) *ed, ing, s*	**which*** (what one? who?) *ever*
weight* (heaviness) *ed, ing, -lifter, s*	**whiff** *ed, ing, s*
weighty *ier, iest, ily, iness*	**while** *d, ǿing, s*
weir *s*	**whilst**
weird *er, est, ly, ness*	**whimper** *ed, ing, er, s*
welcome *d, ǿing, s*	**whine*** (cry; wail) *d, ǿing, r, s*
weld *ed, ing, er, s*	**whip** *ped, ping, per, s*
welfare	**whippet** *s*
well *-behaved, -bred, -wisher, s*	**whirl** *ed, ing, igig, pool, wind, s*
we'll (we shall; we will)	**whisk** *ed, ing, er, s*
wellington boot *s*	**whisker** *ed, y, s*
went	**whisk**y *ies*
wept	**whisper** *ed, ing, er, s*
we're (we are)	**whist** *-drive*
were	**whistle** *d, ǿing, r, s*
weren't (were not)	**white** *r, st, ly, ness, s*
west *ern, erly, ward, wards*	**whiten** *ed, ing, er, s*
wet *ted, ting, ter, test, ly, ness, s*	**whitewash** *ed, ing, es*
we've (we have)	**whiting** *s or* **whiting**
	Whit Sunday *s*
	Whitsun *tide*
wh	**whiz** *zes or* **whizz** *ed, ing, es*
whack *ed, ing, s*	**who** *ever*
whale *ǿing, r, bone, -boat, s*	**who'd** (who had; who would)
wharf *s or* **wharves**	**who'll** (who will; who shall)
what *ever, soever*	**who're** (who are)
what's (what is)	**who's*** (who is)
wheat *-field, -flour, germ, s*	**whom** *soever*
wheedle *d, ǿing, r, s*	**whole*** (all; complete) *sale, some*
wheel *ed, ing, er, barrow, -chair, s*	**wholly*** (completely)
wheeze *d, ǿing, s*	**whoop** *ed, ing, s*
whelk *s*	**whortleberr**y *ies*
when *ever*	**whose*** (belonging to whom)
whence	**why**

ǿ Drop **e** before adding *ing*

weigh	weight	whether	which	whine	who's	whole	wholly
way	wait	weather	witch	wine	whose	hole	holy

wi

wicked	er, est, ly, ness
wicker	work
wicket	-keeper, s
wide	r, st, ly, spread, s
widen	ed, ing, er, s
width	s
widow	ed, ing, er, s
wield	ed, ing, er, s
wife	ly, **wives**
wiggle	d, ∉ing, r, s
wigwam	s
wild	er, est, ly, ness, life, fowl, fire, s
wilderness	es
wilful	ly, ness
will	ed, ing, -power, s
willing	ly, ness
willow	-herb, -tree, -warbler, s
wil y	ier, iest, ily, iness
win	ning, ner, s
wince	d, ∉ing, s
wind (turn; twist)	ing, er, s
wind	ed, ing, -chart, fall, mill, ward, s
wind y	ier, iest, ily, iness
window	-cleaner, -ledge, -pane, -sill, s
windscreen	-wiper, s
wine* (a drink)	d, ∉ing, -bottle, cask, s
wing	ed, ing, er, -span, s
wink	ed, ing, er, s
winkle	d, ∉ing, s
winter	ed, ing, -time, s
wintr y	ier, iest, ily, iness
wipe	d, ∉ing, r, s
wire	d, ∉ing, -netting, -rope, -cutter, s
wireless	ed, ing, es
wir y	ier, iest, ily, iness
wisdom	-tooth, -teeth

wo

wise	r, st, ly
wish	ed, ing, es
wishful	ly, ness
wistful	ly, ness
wit	ted, less, s
witt y	ier, iest, ily, iness
witch* (old woman)	es, craft, -hunt
with	in, out
withdraw	al, ing, n, s
withdrew	
wither	ed, ing, s
withstand	ing, s
withstood	
witness	ed, ing, -box, es
wizard	ry, s
wizened	

wo

wobble	d, ∉ing, r, s
woe	begone, s
woeful	ly, ness
woke	n
wolf	-cub, -pack, **wolves**
woman	hood, ly, **women**
won* (win)	
wonder	ed, ing, ment, land, s
wonderful	ly, ness
won't (will not)	
wood*	ed, man, men, -cutter, land, s
wooden	ly, ness
wood-louse	-lice
woodpecker	s
woodwork	
wool	s
woollen	s
wooll y	ier, iest, iness, ies

∉ Drop e before adding ing

*	wine	witch	won	wood
	whine	which	one (1)	would

wr   x   ya   ye

word	ed, ing, s
wore* (wear)	
work	ed, ing, man, men, shop, er, s
world	-famous, -wide, s
worm	ed, ing, y, eaten, -cast, -hole, s
worn* (wear)	-out
worry	ing
worr ied	ier, ies, isome
worse	
worsen	´ed, ing, s
worst	
worship	ped, ping, per, s
worth	while
worthless	ly, ness
worth y	ier, iest, ily, iness, ies
would* (past of will)	
wouldn't (would not)	
wound (turned; twisted)	
wound (injure)	ed, ing, s
wove	n

· wr

wrangle	d, ∉ing, r, s
wrap* (cover)	ped, ping, per, s
wrath	ful, fully
wreath	s
wreck	age, ed, ing, er, s
wren	s
wrench	ed, ing, es
wrestle	d, ∉ing, r, s
wretch	es
wretched	ly, ness
wriggle	d, ∉ing, r, s
wring* (twist)	ing, er, s
wrinkle	d, ∉ing, r, s
wrist	let, band, s

write* (form letters)	r, s
writing	-case, -desk, -paper, -table, s
written	
writhe	d, ∉ing, s
wrong	ed, ing, ful, ly, ness, s
wrote	
wrung* (twisted)	
wry	er, est, ly, ness

x

X-ray	ed, ing, s
xylophone	s

ya

yacht	ing, sman, smen, -club, s
yak	s
yap	ped, ping, per, s
yard	age, stick, s
yarn	ed, ing, s
yawn	ed, ing, s

ye

year	ly, ling, s
yearn	ed, ing, s
yeast	y
yell	ed, ing, er, s
yellow	er, est, ness, ish, y, s
yelp	ed, ing, er, s
yeo man	men
yes	es
yesterday	s
yet	
yeti	s
yew*	-tree, s

∉ Drop **e** before adding *ing*

* wore	worn	would	wrap	wring	write	wrung	yew
war	warn	wood	rap	ring	right	rung	you
							ewe

yi yu yo ze zi zo zu

---

yi
yield   *ed, ing, s*

yo
yodel   *led, ling, ler, s*
yoga
yog(h)urt
yoke* (wooden bar; join)   *d, eing, s*
yokel   *s*
yolk* (of egg)   *s*
yonder
Yorkshire pudding   *s*
you* (person)
you'd (you had; you would)
you'll (you will)
you're (you are)
you've (you have)
young   *er, est, ish*
youngster   *s*
your
yours
your *self*   *selves*
youth   *-club, s*
youthful   *ly, ness*
yowl   *ed, ing, er, s*

yu
yule   *-log, tide, s*

ze
zeal
zealous   *ly*
zebra   *s*
zebu   *s*
zephyr   *s*
zero   *s*
zest   *ful, fully*

zi
zigzag   *ged, ging, s*
zinc
zip *ped, ping, per, -fastener, s*
zither   *s*

zo
zodiac
zone   *d, eing, s*
zoo   *s*
zoological garden *s*
zoologist   *s*
zoology
zoom   *ed, ing, s*

zu
Zulu   *s*

---

e Drop **e** before adding *ing*

* yoke   you
    yolk   yew
            ewe

Boys' Names

A
Aaron
Adam
Adrian
Alan
Alexander
Alistair
Alfred
Allan
Andrew
Angus
Anthony
Antony
Arthur
Ashley

B
Barry
Benjamin
Bernard
Brendan
Brian
Bryan
Bruce

C
Calvin
Carl
Cedric
Charles
Christian
Christopher
Clifford
Clive
Colin
Courtenay
Craig

D
Dale
Damian
Daniel
Darren
David
Dean
Dennis
Derek
Dominic
Donald
Duncan
Dylan

E
Edmund
Edward
Eric

F
Francis
Frank
Frederick

G
Gareth
Gary
Gavin
Geoffrey
George
Giles
Glen(n)
Glyn
Gordon
Graham
Gregory
Guy

H
Henry
Howard
Hugh

I
Ian
Ivan

J
James
Jamie
Jason
Jeffrey
Jeremy
Jocelyn
John
Jonathan
Joseph
Julian
Justin

K
Karl
Keith
Kenneth
Kevin

L
Lance
Laurence
Lawrence
Lee
Leon
Leonard
Leslie
Luke

M
Malcolm
Marc
Marcus
Mark
Martin
Martyn
Matthew
Maurice
Melvin
Mervyn
Michael
Miles

N
Nathan
Nathaniel
Neil
Neville
Nicholas
Nigel
Noel
Norman

O
Oliver
Owen

P
Patrick
Paul
Peter
Philip
Piers

Q
Quentin

R
Ralph
Randolph
Raymond
Reginald
Rex
Richard
Robert
Robin
Roderick
Rodney
Roger
Roland
Rolf
Ronald
Roy
Royston
Rufus
Rupert
Russell
Ryan

S
Samuel
Scott
Sebastian
Seán
Shane
Shaun
Sidney
Simon
Spencer
Stanley
Stephen
Steven
Stewart
Stuart

T
Terence
Terry
Thomas
Timothy
Tony
Trevor
Tristram

V
Vernon
Victor
Vincent
Vivian

W
Wallace
Walter
Warren
Wayne
Wilfred
William
Winston

Girls' Names

A	C	E	H
Abigail	Cara	Eileen	Hannah
Adele	Carla	Elaine	Hayley
Adrienne	Carol(e)	Eleanor	Hazel
Aileen	Caroline	Elizabeth	Heather
Alexandra	Carolyn	Ellen	Heidi
Alexis	Carrie	Emily	Helen
Alice	Catherine	Emma	Hilary
Alison	Cecilia	Enid	Holly
Amanda	Celia	Erica	
Amelia	Charlotte	Esmé(e)	I
Amy	Charmaine	Estelle	Irene
Andrea	Cheryl	Ester	Isabel
Angela	Chloe	Eveline	
Anita	Christine	Evelyn	J
Ann(e)	Claire		Jacqueline
Anna	Clare	F	Jane
Annabel	Claudia	Fay(e)	Janet
Annabella	Colette	Felicity	Janice
Annette	Corinne	Fiona	Janine
Anthea		Fleur	Jayne
Antonia	D	Frances	Jean
April	Danielle		Jeanette
Audra	Daphne	G	Jennifer
Audrey	Dawn	Gabrielle	Jessica
Averil	Debbie	Gail	Jill
	Deborah	Gayle	Joan
B	Debra	Gaynor	Joanna
Barbara	Deirdre	Gemma	Joanne
Belinda	Delia	Georgina	Johanna
Beryl	Della	Geraldine	Josephine
Betty	Denise	Germaine	Joy
Beverley	Diana	Gillian	Judith
Blanche	Diane	Gina	Julia
Brenda	Dionne	Glenda	Julie
Bridget	Donna	Glynis	June
Bryony	Dorothy	Gwyneth	Justine

K
Karen
Kate
Katharine
Katherine
Kathleen
Kathryn
Katrina
Kay
Keeley
Kelly
Kerry
Kimberly
Kitty
Kirsten
Kirsty

L
Laura
Leanne
Lesley
Linda
Lindsey
Lisa
Lorna
Lorraine
Louisa
Louise
Lucy
Lyndsey
Lynn(e)

M
Madeleine
Mandy
Margaret
Maria

Marie
Martina
Mary
Matilda
Maureen
Maxine
Melanie
Melinda
Melissa
Merle
Michelle
Miranda

N
Nadia
Nadine
Nancy
Naomi
Natalie
Natasha
Nichola
Nicola
Nicole
Nina

O
Olivia

P
Pamela
Patricia
Paula
Pauline
Penelope
Penny
Philippa
Polly

R
Rachael
Rachel
Rebecca
Rebekah
Rita
Rosalie
Rosalind
Rosamund
Rose
Rosemary
Rowena
Ruth

S
Sadie
Sally
Sallyann
Samantha
Sandra
Sara(h)
Sharon
Sheila
Shelley
Shirley
Shona
Sonia
Sophie
Stacey
Stella
Stephanie
Susan
Susannah
Susanne
Suzanne
Sybil
Sylvia

T
Tamara
Tammy
Tamsin
Tania
Tanya
Tara
Teresa
Theresa
Tina
Tracey
Tracy

U
Ursula

V
Valerie
Vanessa
Vicki
Vicky
Victoria
Virginia
Vivien
Vivienne

W
Wendy

Y
Yolande
Yvonne

Z
Zara
Zelda
Zoe

Numbers

	Cardinal		Ordinal				Roman
1	one	s	first	ly,	s	1st	I
2	two	s	second	ly,	s	2nd	II
3	three	s	third	ly,	.s	3rd	III
4	four	s	fourth	ly,	s	4th	IV
5	five	s	fifth	ly,	s	5th	V
6	six	es	sixth	ly,	s	6th	VI
7	seven	s	seventh	ly,	s	7th	VII
8	eight	s	eighth	ly,	s	8th	VIII
9	nine	s	ninth	ly,	s	9th	IX
10	ten	s	tenth	ly,	s	10th	X
11	eleven	s	eleventh		s	11th	XI
12	twelve	s	twelfth		s	12th	XII
13	thirteen	s	thirteenth		s	13th	XIII
14	fourteen	s	fourteenth		s	14th	XIV
15	fifteen	s	fifteenth		s	15th	XV
16	sixteen	s	sixteenth		s	16th	XVI
17	seventeen	s	seventeenth		s	17th	XVII
18	eighteen	s	eighteenth		s	18th	XVIII
19	nineteen	s	nineteenth		s	19th	XIX
20	twent y	ies	twentieth		s	20th	XX
21	twenty-one	s	twenty-first		s	21st	XXI
22	twenty-two	s	twenty-second		s	22nd	XXII
23	twenty-three	s	twenty-third		s	23rd	XXIII
24	twenty-four	s	twenty-fourth		s	24th	XXIV
25	twenty-five	s	twenty-fifth		s	25th	XXV
26	twenty-six	es	twenty-sixth		s	26th	XXVI
27	twenty-seven	s	twenty-seventh		s	27th	XXVII
28	twenty-eight	s	twenty-eighth		s	28th	XXVIII
29	twenty-nine	s	twenty-ninth		s	29th	XXIX
30	thirt y	ies	thirtieth		s	30th	XXX
31	thirty-one	s	thirty-first		s	31st	XXXI
40	fort y	ies	fortieth		s	40th	XL
41	forty-one	s	forty-first		s	41st	XLI

	Cardinal		Ordinal			Roman
50	fift *y*	*ies*	fiftieth	*s*	50th	L
51	fifty-one	*s*	fifty-first	*s*	51st	LI
60	sixt *y*	*ies*	sixtieth	*s*	60th	LX
61	sixty-one	*s*	sixty-first	*s*	61st	LXI
70	sevent *y*	*ies*	seventieth	*s*	70th	LXX
71	seventy-one	*s*	seventy-first	*s*	71st	LXXI
80	eight *y*	*ies*	eightieth	*s*	80th	LXXX
81	eighty-one	*s*	eighty-first	*s*	81st	LXXXI
90	ninet *y*	*ies*	ninetieth	*s*	90th	XC
91	ninety-one	*s*	ninety-first	*s*	91st	XCI
100	hundred	*s*	hundredth	*s*	100th	C
500	five hundred		five hundreth		500th	D
1,000	thousand	*s*	thousandth	*s*	1,000th	M
10,000	ten thousand		ten thousandth		10,000th	
100,000	one hundred thousand		one hundred thousandth		100,000th	
1,000,000	million	*s*	millionth	*s*	1,000,000th	

Roman numerals

When a smaller number comes *before* a larger one, it is subtracted,
e.g. IV = 5 − 1 = 4; IX = 10 − 1 = 9; XL = 50 − 10 = 40; CD = 500 − 100 = 400

When a smaller number comes *after* a larger one, it is added,
e.g. VI = 5 + 1 = 6; XI = 10 + 1 = 11; LX = 50 + 10 = 60; DC = 500 + 100 = 600

Countries and Peoples of the World

Afghanistan	Afghan	s	Ecuador	Ecuadorean	s
Albania	Albanian	s	Egypt	Egyptian	s
Algeria	Algerian	s	England	English *(plural)*	
America (see United States of America)			Ethiopia	Ethiopian	s
Angola	Angolan	s			
Argentina	Argentinian	s	Falkland Islands	Falkland Islander	s
Australia	Australian	s	Fiji	Fijian	s
Austria	Austrian	s	Finland	Finn	s
			France	French *(plural)*	
Bangladesh	Bangladeshi	s			
Belarus (see Belorussia)			Gambia	Gambian	s
Belgium	Belgian	s	Germany	German	s
Belorussia	Belorussian	s	Ghana	Ghanaian	s
Benin	Beninese		Great Britain (see Britain)		
Bhutan	Bhutanese		Greece	Greek	s
Bolivia	Bolivian	s	Guatemala	Guatemalan	s
Botswana	Citizen of Botswana		Guinea	Guinean	s
			Guyana	Guyanese	
Brazil	Brazilian	s			
Britain	British *(plural)* or Briton	s	Haiti	Haitian	s
Bulgaria	Bulgarian	s	Holland (see Netherlands)		
Burma (now called *Myanmar*)	Burmese		Honduras	Honduran	s
			Hong Kong	Inhabitant of Hong Kong	
			Hungary	Hungarian	s
Cambodia	Cambodian	s	Iceland	Icelander	s
Cameroon	Cameroonian	s	India	Indian	s
Canada	Canadian	s	Indonesia	Indonesian	s
Central African Republic	Person of the Central African Republic		Iran	Iranian	s
			Iraq	Iraqi	s
			Ireland, Republic of	Irish *(plural)*	
Chad	Chadian	s	Israel	Israeli	s
Chile	Chilean	s	Italy	Italian	s
China	Chinese				
Colombia	Colombian	s	Jamaica	Jamaican	s
Congo	Congolese		Japan	Japanese	
Costa Rica	Costa Rican	s	Jordan	Jordanian	s
Cuba	Cuban	s			
Cyprus	Cypriot	s	Kazakhstan	Kazakh	s
Czech Republic	Czech	s	Kenya	Kenyan	s
			Korea (North, South)	Korean	s
Denmark	Dane	s			

Kuwait	Kuwaiti	s
Lebanon	Lebanese	
Liberia	Liberian	s
Libya	Libyan	s
Luxembourg	Luxembourger	s
Madagascar	**Malagasy** *Malagasies*	
Malawi	Malawian	s
Malaysia	Malaysian	s
Mali	Malian	s
Mauritania	Mauritanian	s
Mauritius	Mauritian	s
Mexico	Mexican	s
Moldavia, Moldova	Moldavian	s
Monaco	Monégasque	s
Mongolia	Mongolian	s
Morocco	Moroccan	s
Mozambique	Mozambican	s
Myanmar (until 1989 called *Burma*)		
Namibia	Namibian	s
Nepal	Nepalese	
Netherlands	Dutch *(plural)*	
New Zealand	New Zealander	s
Nicaragua	Nicaraguan	s
Niger	Nigerien	s
Nigeria	Nigerian	s
Norway	Norwegian	s
Oman	Omani	s
Pakistan	Pakistani	s
Panama	Panamanian	s
Papua New Guinea	Papua New Guinean	s
Paraguay	Paraguayan	s
Peru	Peruvian	s
Philippines	Filipino	s
Poland	Pole	s
Portugal	Portuguese	
Romania	Romanian	s
Russia	Russian	s
Saudi Arabia	Saudi Arabian	s
Scotland	Scot	s
Senegal	Senegalese	

Sierra Leone	Sierra Leonean	s
Singapore	Singaporean	s
Slovakia	Slovak	s
Somalia	Somali	s
South Africa	South African	s
Spain	Spanish *(plural)*, Spaniard	s
Sri Lanka	Sri Lankan	s
Sudan	Sudanese	
Sweden	Swede	s
Switzerland	Swiss	
Syria	Syrian	s
Tanzania	Tanzanian	s
Thailand	Thai	s
Trinidad and Tobago	Trinidadian and Tobagan or Tobagonian	s
Tunisia	Tunisian	s
Turkey	Turk	s
Uganda	Ugandan	s
Ukraine	Ukrainian	s
Union of Soviet Socialist Republics (until 1991)	Russian	s
United Arab Emirates	Person of the United Arab Emirates	
United Kingdom	British *(plural)*	
United States of America	American	s
Uruguay	Uruguayan	s
Uzbekistan	Uzbek	s
Venezuela	Venezuelan	s
Vietnam	Vietnamese	
Wales	Welsh *(plural)*	
Yemen, Republic of	Yemeni	s
Zaïre	Zaïrean	s
Zambia	Zambian	s
Zimbabwe	Zimbabwean	s

Parts of Speech

Noun: A naming word, e.g. *boy, man, cat, house, Susan, England*.
On *Monday John* went by *coach* to *London Zoo* with his
teacher, Mr. Smith, and other *children* from his *class*.

Pronoun: A word used instead of a noun, e.g. *me, she, it, we, us, him*.
You and *I* will go now and *he* can come later with *them*.

Adjective: A word that is 'added to' a noun to describe it, e.g.
fat, thin, big, brown, green, ugly, pretty, delicious.
A *funny, little, old* man with a *large* nose and a *grey*
beard showed the *small* children his *beautiful* garden.

Verb: A doing word; a word that tells what is done, e.g.
do, go, stay, talk, shout, jump, lift, fight, eat, drink.
Stop running or you will *fall* and *hurt* yourself.

Adverb: A word that tells how, when or where something happens, e.g.
soon, often, there, now, never, quickly, carefully, carelessly.
Yesterday when I came *here* I jumped *over* that wall.

Preposition: A word that is placed before a noun, e.g.
by, in, into, at, for, under, over, against, near.
Bob went *with* his sister *on* a bus *to* the town.

Conjunction: A word that joins sentences, phrases or words, e.g.
or, than, though, although, because, while, unless.
John *and* Mary will go *if* it is fine *but* not *if* it rains.

Interjection: A word used as an exclamation, e.g. *Ah! Alas! Hey!*
Oh! You did frighten me. *Ouch!* That hurt.

Article: One of the three words – *a, an* or *the*.
A boy rode on *an* elephant at *the* zoo.

Spelling Lists of Words to Learn

The following lists contain the words you will need to use most often in your writing and compositions. You should, therefore, learn and try to remember how to spell all these words. Choose the shortest and easiest words at the beginning of each section to learn first. It is better to learn a few words each day rather than a long list, at one time, once a week. To make it easier for you the words are usually arranged in lists according to the number of letters in the words: three, four, five letters, etc. The number at the top of a word list shows the number of letters in each word in that list. Before you start to learn a list of words first study all the words in the list and notice that some words have the same letters in exactly the same order as others in the list.

All the words on pages 118 to 123 and at the bottom of page 126 are verbs, or may be used as verbs, and are arranged in lists according to the way in which their *ed, ing, s* endings are formed. When your teacher tests you on the words you have learnt he/she will probably ask you how to spell some of these words with their *ed, ing, s* endings to see whether you have understood this, e.g.

bark	**scare**	**drop**
mark *ed*	**score** *d*	**chop** *ped*
park *ing*	**stor** *ing*	**shop** *ping*
work *s*	**stone** *s*	**stop** *s*

You may add *ed, ing, s* to all the following words, e.g.
camp *ed, ing, s* = **camped, camping, camps**

3		4		4		4	
act	*ed, ing, s*	**book**	*ed, ing, s*	**back**	*ed, ing, s*	**camp**	*ed, ing, s*
add		cook		pack		damp	
air		hook		sack		bump	
arm		look		dock		dump	
ask		cool		lock		jump	
end		pool		rock		lump	
ink		show		kick		pump	
oil		slow		lick		bomb	
own		flow		pick		comb	
toy		snow		tick		lamb	

4		4		4		4	
dust	*ed, ing, s*	**call**	*ed, ing, s*	**bark**	*ed, ing, s*	**load**	*ed, ing, s*
last		fell		mark		boat	
list		well		park		coat	
nest		yell		work		roar	
rest		fill		cork		soap	
test		kill		fork		help	
post		mill		milk		long	
lift		will		talk		hunt	
melt		pull		walk		want	
salt		roll		bank		word	

4		4		4		4	
form	*ed, ing, s*	**gain**	*ed, ing, s*	**head**	*ed, ing, s*	**bath**	*ed, ing, s*
farm		pain		heal		down	
harm		rain		heat		even	
warm		pair		seat		open	
band		fail		fear		turn	
hand		jail		near		join	
land		nail		team		iron	
sand		sail		play		part	
bang		tail		pray		mind	
gang		wait		stay		view	

5		5		5		6	
clean	ed, ing, s	knock	ed, ing, s	thank	ed, ing, s	answer	ed, ing, s
clear		clock		train		corner	
climb		block		tramp		flower	
cloud		shock		treat		bother	
clown		black		light		gather	
chain		crack		right		matter	
chair		track		sight		master	
chalk		brick		dream		murder	
cheer		trick		radio		number	
cheat		wreck		visit		wonder	

5		5		6		6	
enter	ed, ing, s	count	ed, ing, s	appear	ed, ing, s	remind	ed, ing, s
cover		cough		arrest		return	
lower		rough		attack		reward	
offer		round		happen		school	
order		pound		hollow		scream	
water		sound		follow		stream	
paper		mouth		borrow		belong	
paint		group		button		poison	
point		scout		butter		powder	
plant		shout		letter		obtain	

5		5		6		7	
laugh	ed, ing, s	boast	ed, ing, s	colour	ed, ing, s	explain	ed, ing, s
haunt		coast		doctor		contain	
field		roast		ground		curtain	
float		toast		garden		captain	
floor		start		awaken		holiday	
flood		stamp		fasten		journey	
bloom		storm		listen		present	
stoop		allow		pocket		pretend	
spoon		enjoy		rocket		soldier	
sport		guard		ticket		station	

5		6+		6+		7+	
crawl	ed, ing, s	expect	ed, ing, s	repair	ed, ing, s	disobey	ed, ing, s
creak		collect		remain		discover	
crowd		correct		remind		disappear	
crown		protect		remember		disappoint	

You may add *ing* and *s* to the following words. You may not add *ed*. The words on the right of the columns are used instead.

buy	*ing, s* :	**bought**	**wear**	*ing, s* :	**wore, worn**
lay	:	**laid**	**ring**	:	**rang, rung**
pay	:	**paid**	**sing**	:	**sang, sung**
say	:	**said**	**spring**	:	**sprang, sprung**
cost	:	**cost**	**sink**	:	**sank, sunk**
feed	:	**fed**	**drink**	:	**drank, drunk**
feel	:	**felt**	**think**	:	**thought**
find	:	**found**	**bring**	:	**brought**
hear	:	**heard**	**fight**	:	**fought**
hold	:	**held**	**build**	:	**built**
hurt	*ing, s* :	**hurt**	**shoot**	*ing, s* :	**shot**
keep	:	**kept**	**sleep**	:	**slept**
lead	:	**led**	**stand**	:	**stood**
lend	:	**lent**	**spend**	:	**spent**
send	:	**sent**	**sweep**	:	**swept**
sell	:	**sold**	**swing**	:	**swung**
tell	:	**told**	**spread**	:	**spread**
meet	:	**met**	**break**	:	**broke,** *n*
mean	:	**meant**	**speak**	:	**spoke,** *n*
read	:	**read**	**steal**	:	**stole,** *n*
see	*n, ing, s* :	**saw**	**eat**	*en, ing, s* :	**ate**
blow	*n, ing, s* :	**blew**	**beat**	*en, ing, s* :	**beat**
draw	*n, ing, s* :	**drew**	**fall**	*en, ing, s* :	**fell**
grow	*n, ing, s* :	**grew**			
know	*n, ing, s* :	**knew**	**catch**	*ing, es* :	**caught**
throw	*n, ing, s* :	**threw**	**teach**	*ing, es* :	**taught**

You may add *ed, ing, es* to all the following words:

box *ed, ing, es*	**fish** *ed, ing, es*	**kiss** *ed, ing, es*	**fetch** *ed, ing, es*
fix	**dish**	**miss**	**match**
mix	**push**	**cross**	**watch**
	rush	**pass**	**scratch**
	wash	**class**	**march**
	wish	**grass**	**reach**
	brush	**guess**	**bunch**
	crash	**press**	**lunch**
	flash	**dress**	**touch**
	finish	**address**	**search**

All the following words end in a consonant followed by a letter **e**.
You may add *d* and *s* to all the words but the **e** must be dropped before adding *ing*, e.g.
  hope *d, ∉ing, s* = **hoped, hoping, hopes**

4		4		4		5	
care *d, ∉ing, s*		**dive** *d, ∉ing, s*		**hope** *d, ∉ing, s*		**argue** *d, ∉ing, s*	
dare		**tire**		**rope**		**blame**	
face		**fire**		**note**		**flame**	
race		**wire**		**hole**		**place**	
save		**wipe**		**love**		**dance**	
wave		**fine**		**move**		**piece**	
hate		**line**		**name**		**force**	
bake		**live**		**side**		**voice**	
rake		**like**		**time**		**price**	
wake		**hike**		**type**		**prize**	

∉ Drop **e** before adding *ing*

continued on page 122

5		5		6		6	
chase	d, ∉ing, s	**scare**	d, ∉ing, s	**battle**	d, ∉ing, s	**arrive**	d, ∉ing, s
close		**score**		**bottle**		**behave**	
cause		**store**		**settle**		**chance**	
pause		**stone**		**bubble**		**bridge**	
house		**smile**		**paddle**		**change**	
amuse		**serve**		**puzzle**		**charge**	
raise		**taste**		**bundle**		**garage**	
nurse		**waste**		**double**		**damage**	
sense		**brave**		**hurdle**		**manage**	
tease		**prove**		**single**		**voyage**	

6		7		7		8	
decide	d, ∉ing, s	**balance**	d, ∉ing, s	**picture**	d, ∉ing, s	**surprise**	d, ∉ing, s
divide		**bandage**		**promise**		**exercise**	
invite		**believe**		**provide**		**exchange**	
escape		**bicycle**		**prepare**		**celebrate**	
notice		**breathe**		**produce**		**continue**	
excuse		**deserve**		**grumble**		**decorate**	
refuse		**capture**		**stumble**		**describe**	
rescue		**explore**		**tremble**		**puncture**	
circle		**imagine**		**trouble**		**struggle**	
centre		**receive**		**whistle**		**treasure**	

All the words in the left-hand columns end in a consonant followed by a letter **e**. You may add s to all the words but the **e** must be dropped before adding *ing*.

You may not add *d*. The words on the right of the column are used instead.

come	∉ing, s : **came**	**bite**	∉ing, s : **bit, bitten**
make	: **made**	**hide**	: **hid, hidden**
lose	: **lost**	**ride**	: **rode, ridden**
leave	: **left**	**rise**	: **rose, risen**
slide	: **slid**	**drive**	: **drove, driven**
strike	: **struck**	**write**	: **wrote, written**
		choose	: **chose, n**

give	n, ∉ing, s : **gave**
take	n, ∉ing, s : **took**
shake	n, ∉ing, s : **shook**
mistake	n, ∉ing, s : **mistook**

∉ Drop **e** before adding *ing*

You may add *s* to all the following words. The final consonant (the last letter) must be doubled before adding *ed, ing,* e.g.

drop   *ped, ping. s* = **dropped, dropping, drops**

3		3		3		4	
bat	*ted, ting, s*	**dip**	*ped, ping, s*	**beg**	*ged, ging, s*	**drop**	*ped, ping, s*
pat		**rip**		**peg**		**chop**	
pet		**tip**		**gag**		**shop**	
net		**zip**		**wag**		**stop**	
wet		**hop**		**hug**		**swop**	
fit		**pop**		**tug**		**ship**	
rot		**top**		**gun**		**slip**	
rob		**tap**		**sun**		**skip**	
mob		**map**		**pin**		**drip**	
sob		**yap**		**jab**		**grip**	

4		4		5+		5+	
trip	*ped. ping. s*	**plan**	*ned, ning. s*	**equal**	*led, ling. s*	**admit**	*ted, ting, s*
whip		**stun**		**signal**		**permit**	
clap		**grin**		**pencil**		**commit**	
snap		**skin**		**model**		**regret**	
trap		**skid**		**cancel**		**occur**	
wrap		**chat**		**parcel**		**refer**	
step		**plot**		**shovel**		**prefer**	
stab		**knot**		**travel**		**equip**	
grab		**knit**		**tunnel**		**kidnap**	
drag		**dial**		**quarrel**		**unwrap**	

None of the following words may end in *ed*.
The words in the right hand column are used instead.

get	*ting, s* : **got**		**dig**	*ging, s* : **dug**		
set	*ting, s* : **set**		**run**	*ning, s* : **ran**		
sit	*ting, s* : **sat**		**win**	*ning, s* : **won**		
hit	*ting, s* : **hit**		**spin**	*ning, s* : **spun**		
cut	*ting, s* : **cut**		**begin**	*ning, s* : **began, begun**		
shut	*ting. s* : **shut**		**swim**	*ming, s* : **swam, swum**		

You may add *er, est, ly, ness* to all the following words, e.g.
bold *er, est, ly, ness* = **bolder, boldest, boldly, boldness**

4		4+		5	
bold	*er, est, ly, ness*	**fair**	*er, est, ly, ness*	**light**	*er, est, ly, ness*
cold		**dear**		**tight**	
poor		**near**		**quick**	
cool		**neat**		**quiet**	
deep		**mean**		**queer**	
dark		**weak**		**steep**	
kind		**clean**		**sharp**	
loud		**clear**		**short**	
rich		**cheap**		**smart**	
slow		**great**		**thick**	
soft		**fresh**		**rough**	
wild		**clever**		**tough**	

You may add *r, st, ly, ness* to the following words:

4		4+	
late	*r, st, ly, ness*	**rude**	*r, st, ly, ness*
nice		**wide**	
fine		**large**	
safe		**close**	
sore		**fierce**	
sure		**strange**	

You may add *ly, ness* to the following words but
the last letter must be doubled before adding *er, est*.

3		3+	
sad	*der, dest, ly, ness*	**fat**	*ter, test*
mad	*der, dest*	**flat**	*ter, test*
hot	*ter, test*	**thin**	*ner, nest*
fit	*ter, test*		

All the following words end in *y*.
The *y* must be dropped before adding *ier, iest, ily, iness*, e.g.

    eas *y   ier, iest, ily, iness* = **easier, easiest, easily, easiness**

4+

eas *y   ier, iest, ily, iness*
laz *y*
tid *y*
tin *y*
ugl *y*
dirt *y*
empt *y*
heav *y*
juic *y*
luck *y*
nois *y*
rock *y*

5

happ *y ier, iest, ily, iness*
sunn *y*
funn *y*
fuss *y*
mess *y*
mudd *y*
joll *y*
sill *y*
sorr *y*
shak *y*
wear *y*
wind *y*

6

stick *y ier, iest, ily, iness*
trick *y*
shabb *y*
prett *y*
lovel *y*
lonel *y*
sleep *y*
greed *y*
cheek *y*
breez *y*
gloom *y*
storm *y*

6+

hungr *y ier, iest, ily, iness*
cloud *y*
clums *y*
chill *y*
kindl *y*
stead *y*
untid *y*
unluck *y*
naught *y*
thirst *y*
health *y*
wealth *y*

4+

bus *y   ier, iest, ily*
angr *y   ier, iest, ily*
earl *y   ier, iest, iness*
sand *y   ier, iest, iness*
merr *y   ier, iest, ily, iment*

dough	also	Monday	January
cough	always	Tuesday	February
rough	almost	Wednesday	March
tough	although	Thursday	April
enough	already	Friday	May
plough	altogether	Saturday	June
through		Sunday	July
ought	all right		August
bought		spring	September
brought		summer	October
fought		autumn	November
thought		winter	December

All the following words end in **y**.
You may add *ing* but the **y** must be dropped before adding *ied, ies*.

cry	*ing*	**carry**	*ing*	**copy**	*ing*
cried	*ies*	**carr**ied	*ies*	**cop**ied	*ies*
dry	*ing*	**marry**	*ing*	**bury**	*ing*
dried	*ies*	**marr**ied	*ies*	**bur**ied	*ies*
try	*ing*	**hurry**	*ing*	**tidy**	*ing*
tried	*ies*	**hurr**ied	*ies*	**tid**ied	*ies*
fry	*ing*	**worry**	*ing*	**occupy**	*ing*
fried	*ies*	**worr**ied	*ies*	**occup**ied	*ies*
spy	*ing*	**empty**	*ing*	**satisfy**	*ing*
spied	*ies*	**empt**ied	*ies*	**satisf**ied	*ies*
fly	*ing*	**study**	*ing*	**terrify**	*ing*
flies		**stud**ied	*ies*	**terrif**ied	*ies*
flew, flown					

A very few verbs end in **ie**. You may add *d* and *s* but the **ie** must be changed to *y* before adding *ing*.

die	*d, s*	**lie**	*d, s*	**tie**	*d, s*
dying		**ly**ing		**ty**ing	

Singular		Plural	Singular	Plural	Singular	Plural
foot		feet	bab*y*	*ies*	key	*s*
goose		geese	lad*y*	*ies*	donkey	*s*
tooth		teeth	bod*y*	*ies*	monkey	*s*
mouse		mice	pon*y*	*ies*	valley	*s*
man		men	cit*y*	*ies*	chimney	*s*
woman		women	arm*y*	*ies*	cowboy	*s*
child		children	nav*y*	*ies*	railway	*s*
			aunt*y*	*ies*	gangway	*s*
life		lives	dadd*y*	*ies*	holiday	*s*
wife		wives	mumm*y*	*ies*	birthday	*s*
knife		knives				
			dais*y*	*ies*	zoo	*s*
leaf		leaves	dair*y*	*ies*	piano	*s*
loaf		loaves	fair*y*	*ies*	radio	*s*
thief		thieves	stor*y*	*ies*		
			part*y*	*ies*	hero	*es*
dwarf	*s* or	dwarves	jell*y*	*ies*	cargo	*es*
scarf	*s* or	scarves	lorr*y*	*ies*	Negro	*es*
wharf	*s* or	wharves	pupp*y*	*ies*	potato	*es*
hoof	*s* or	hooves	hobb*y*	*ies*	tomato	*es*
roof	*s*		enem*y*	*ies*	volcano	*es*
elf		elves	canar*y*	*ies*	bus	*es*
calf		calves	famil*y*	*ies*	glass	*es*
half		halves	grann*y*	*ies*	beach	*es*
wolf		wolves	cherr*y*	*ies*	peach	*es*
shelf		shelves	countr*y*	*ies*	torch	*es*
			librar*y*	*ies*	witch	*es*
self		selves	factor*y*	*ies*	church	*es*
itself			robber*y*	*ies*	circus	*es*
myself			myster*y*	*ies*	princess	*es*
himself			discover*y*	*ies*	sandwich	*es*
herself						
yourself		yourselves	**every**	*body, one, thing, where*		
		ourselves	**any**	*body, one, thing, where, how, way*		
		themselves	**some**	*body, one, thing, where, how, times*		

4	4	5	4		4		5
able	than	these	bell	s	bird	s	giant
away	that	those	ball	s	desk	s	glove
best	then	where	wall	s	lake	s	green
born	them	which	hall	s	lawn	s	hedge
both	they	while	hill	s	lion	s	horse
does	this	whole	cake	s	neck	s	hotel
done	true	whose	card	s	nose	s	jewel
goes	luck	worse	cart	s	page	s	lemon
gone	ever	worst	cave	s	path	s	noise
gold	very	worth	case	s	pond	s	ocean

4	4	5	4		4		5
dead	went	could	coal	s	shed	s	other
deaf	were	would	goal	s	shoe	s	owner
each	what	magic	door	s	sock	s	plate
else	when	might	food	s	song	s	fruit
just	with	money	moon	s	tent	s	pupil
must	clay	music	room	s	town	s	purse
much	beef	never	wood	s	tree	s	queen
many	pork	pence	wool	s	mile	s	salad
more	east	sugar	flag	s	your	s	shirt
most	west	ready	frog	s	year	s	snake

4	5	5	4		5		5
from	about	among	game	s	apple	s	stair
next	above	below	gate	s	baker	s	stick
none	after	blood	gift	s	bread	s	stove
only	again	earth	hole	s	beast	s	sword
once	ahead	often	home	s	cabin	s	table
upon	alone	sorry	hour	s	cloth	s	thing
same	along	sheep	king	s	comic	s	tiger
some	alike	shall	kite	s	dozen	s	truck
soon	alive	under	knee	s	front	s	white
such	aside	until	idea	s	ghost	s	world

6	7	6		6		9	
across	against	friend	s	infant	s	adventure	s
afraid	another	forest	s	insect	s	aeroplane	s
around	because	finger	s	inside	s	afternoon	s
asleep	beneath	father	s	island	s	chocolate	s
ashore	between	mother	s	desert	s	favourite	s
awhile	clothes	leader	s	orange	s	passenger	s
before	instead	reader	s	second	s	newspaper	s
behind	nothing	saucer	s	minute	s	orchestra	s
better	perhaps	sister	s	moment	s	programme	s
cattle	without	reason	s	museum	s	vegetable	s

6	8	6		7		full	y
during	together	bullet	s	bedroom	s	awful	ly
either	tomorrow	carrot	s	blanket	s	useful	ly
famous	horrible	coffee	s	brother	s	careful	ly
hardly	horribly	cotton	s	teacher	s	playful	ly
little	terrible	dinner	s	sausage	s	cheerful	ly
middle	terribly	kitten	s	cabbage	s	dreadful	ly
modern	possible	lesson	s	cottage	s	thankful	ly
unless	possibly	rabbit	s	message	s	beautiful	ly
utmost	probable	robber	s	village	s	forgetful	ly
within	probably	rubber	s	lettuce	s	wonderful	ly

6	6		6		7			
people	animal	s	parent	s	chicken	s	helpful	ly
petrol	banana	s	person	s	kitchen	s	hopeful	ly
plenty	beside	s	prince	s	husband	s	skilful	ly
police	bucket	s	secret	s	pudding	s	faithful	ly
rather	castle	s	street	s	morning	s	grateful	ly
really	cousin	s	string	s	evening	s	peaceful	ly
safety	coward	s	violin	s	tadpole	s	powerful	ly
should	danger	s	window	s	tractor	s	spiteful	ly
seldom	engine	s	pillow	s	visitor	s	delightful	ly
silver	needle	s	yellow	s	outside	s	disgraceful	ly

Contractions *(shortened words)*

These are words which have been shortened by joining two words together and placing an apostrophe where a letter or letters have been left out. Learn the words and the contractions, being very careful to remember exactly where the apostrophe goes.

can't = cannot
don't = do not
won't = will not
isn't = is not
aren't = are not
didn't = did not
hadn't = had not
hasn't = has not
wasn't = was not
shan't = shall not
doesn't = does not
haven't = have not
mustn't = must not
needn't = need not
weren't = were not
couldn't = could not
wouldn't = would not
shouldn't = should not

he's = he is;   he has
she's = she is;   she has
it's = it is
who's = who is
that's = that is
what's = what is
here's = here is
there's = there is

I'll = I will;   I shall
we'll = we will;   we shall
he'll = he will;   he shall
she'll = she will;   she shall
you'll = you will;   you shall
who'll = who will;   who shall
they'll = they will;   they shall

I'd = I had;   I would
he'd = he had;   he would
we'd = we had;   we would
you'd = you had;   you would
who'd = who had;   who would
they'd = they had;   they would

we're = we are
you're = you are
who're = who are
they're = they are

I've = I have
we've = we have
you've = you have
they've = they have

I'm = I am

The apostrophe is also used to show possession, e.g.

The boy's book;   girl's coat;   man's car;   woman's watch.
The boys' books;   girls' coats;   men's cars;   women's watches.

Homophones

These are words that sound alike but have different meanings and spellings.

arc	(curve)	**pain**	(suffering)	**accept**	(receive)
ark	(boat; box)	**pane**	(of glass)	**except**	(leaving out)
beach	(seashore)	**pair**	(two)	**allowed**	(let; permitted)
beech	(tree)	**pear**	(fruit)	**aloud**	(loudly)
bean	(plant)	**peace**	(quiet)	**altar**	(church table)
been	(past of be)	**piece**	(a part)	**alter**	(change)
blew	(blow)	**peer**	(stare)	**dear**	(beloved; costly)
blue	(colour)	**pier**	(jetty)	**deer**	(animal)
bough	(branch)	**place**	(position)	**flour**	(ground wheat)
bow	(bend)	**plaice**	(fish)	**flower**	(blossom)
brake	(to stop)	**rap**	(knock)	**foul**	(dirty; unfair)
break	(to snap)	**wrap**	(cover)	**fowl**	(bird)
chute	(a slide)	**sail**	(ship)	**freeze**	(ice; cold)
shoot	(fire)	**sale**	(selling)	**frieze**	(wall decoration)
die	(lose life)	**slay**	(kill)	**groan**	(moan)
dye	(colour)	**sleigh**	(sled)	**grown**	(got bigger)
farther	(further)	**stair**	(step)	**guessed**	(did guess)
father	(parent)	**stare**	(look at)	**guest**	(visitor)
fort	(castle)	**steal**	(thieve)	**hear**	(listen)
fought	(fight)	**steel**	(metal)	**here**	(in this place)
hair	(of head)	**tail**	(end)	**heard**	(listened)
hare	(animal)	**tale**	(story)	**herd**	(of cattle, etc.)
hart	(stag)	**pail**	(bucket)	**hoard**	(hidden store)
heart	(of body)	**pale**	(whitish)	**horde**	(crowd)
heal	(cure)	**scene**	(view; place)	**hour**	(sixty minutes)
heel	(of foot)	**seen**	(noticed)	**our**	(belonging to us)
higher	(taller)	**tire**	(weary)	**hole**	(hollow place)
hire	(rent)	**tyre**	(wheel cover)	**whole**	(all; complete)
hoarse	(husky)	**weak**	(not strong)	**meat**	(flesh)
horse	(animal)	**week**	(seven days)	**meet**	(come together)
leant	(leaned)	**weather**	(climate)	**meter**	(measuring box)
lent	(lend)	**whether**	(if)	**metre**	(length measure)
made	(make)	**wood**	(timber)	**moan**	(groan)
maid	(girl)	**would**	(past of will)	**mown**	(cut grass, etc.)
muscle	(of body)	**won**	(did win)	**signet**	(seal, ring)
mussel	(shellfish)	**one**	(single)	**cygnet**	(young swan)

knew	(know)	**shore**	(seashore)
new	(just made)	**sure**	(certain)
knight	(Sir)	**their**	(belonging to them)
night	(opp. of day)	**there**	(in that place)
know	(understand)	**they're**	(they are)
no	(not any; opp. of yes)	**theirs**	(belonging to them)
knot	(tied string, etc.)	**there's**	(there is)
not	(no)	**threw**	(throw)
passed	(did pass)	**through**	(from end to end)
past	(time gone by)	**throne**	(king's seat)
ring	(circle; bell sound)	**thrown**	(throw)
wring	(twist)	**board**	(wood; go on ship; lodge)
wait	(stay; serve)	**bored**	(weary; drilled hole)
weight	(Heaviness)	**cereal**	(wheat, oats, etc.)
way	(direction)	**serial**	(in parts)
weigh	(measure heaviness)	**currant**	(fruit)
waste	(not used; useless)	**current**	(flow of water, air, etc.)
waist	(of body)	**cue**	(hint; billiard-stick)
which	(what one? who?)	**queue**	(line of persons, etc.)
witch	(old woman)	**fair**	(just; light; entertainment)
who's	(who is)	**fare**	(price of journey; food)
whose	(belonging to whom?)	**core**	(middle of apple, etc.)
you're	(you are)	**corps**	(group of cadets, etc.)
your	(belonging to you)	**road**	(highway)
it's	(it is)	**rode**	(ride)
its	(belonging to it)	**rowed**	(used oars)
pedal	(foot lever)	**cent**	(coin)
peddle	(to hawk goods)	**sent**	(send)
hall	(room; passage)	**scent**	(smell; perfume)
haul	(pull; amount taken)	**rain**	(water)
him	(he)	**reign**	(rule)
hymn	(song of praise)	**rein**	(strap)
mare	(female horse)	**buy**	(purchase)
mayor	(head of town or city)	**by**	(near to, etc.)
medal	(badge – for bravery, etc.)	**bye**	(a run)
meddle	(interfere)	**to**	(towards)
pray	(ask God)	**too**	(also; more than enough)
prey	(victim; thing hunted)	**two**	(number)

Multiplication Tables

0 × 2 = 0	0 × 3 = 0	0 × 4 = 0	0 × 5 = 0
1 × 2 = 2	1 × 3 = 3	1 × 4 = 4	1 × 5 = 5
2 × 2 = 4	2 × 3 = 6	2 × 4 = 8	2 × 5 = 10
3 × 2 = 6	3 × 3 = 9	3 × 4 = 12	3 × 5 = 15
4 × 2 = 8	4 × 3 = 12	4 × 4 = 16	4 × 5 = 20
5 × 2 = 10	5 × 3 = 15	5 × 4 = 20	5 × 5 = 25
6 × 2 = 12	6 × 3 = 18	6 × 4 = 24	6 × 5 = 30
7 × 2 = 14	7 × 3 = 21	7 × 4 = 28	7 × 5 = 35
8 × 2 = 16	8 × 3 = 24	8 × 4 = 32	8 × 5 = 40
9 × 2 = 18	9 × 3 = 27	9 × 4 = 36	9 × 5 = 45
10 × 2 = 20	10 × 3 = 30	10 × 4 = 40	10 × 5 = 50
11 × 2 = 22	11 × 3 = 33	11 × 4 = 44	11 × 5 = 55
12 × 2 = 24	12 × 3 = 36	12 × 4 = 48	12 × 5 = 60

0 × 6 = 0	0 × 7 = 0	0 × 8 = 0	0 × 9 = 0
1 × 6 = 6	1 × 7 = 7	1 × 8 = 8	1 × 9 = 9
2 × 6 = 12	2 × 7 = 14	2 × 8 = 16	2 × 9 = 18
3 × 6 = 18	3 × 7 = 21	3 × 8 = 24	3 × 9 = 27
4 × 6 = 24	4 × 7 = 28	4 × 8 = 32	4 × 9 = 36
5 × 6 = 30	5 × 7 = 35	5 × 8 = 40	5 × 9 = 45
6 × 6 = 36	6 × 7 = 42	6 × 8 = 48	6 × 9 = 54
7 × 6 = 42	7 × 7 = 49	7 × 8 = 56	7 × 9 = 63
8 × 6 = 48	8 × 7 = 56	8 × 8 = 64	8 × 9 = 72
9 × 6 = 54	9 × 7 = 63	9 × 8 = 72	9 × 9 = 81
10 × 6 = 60	10 × 7 = 70	10 × 8 = 80	10 × 9 = 90
11 × 6 = 66	11 × 7 = 77	11 × 8 = 88	11 × 9 = 99
12 × 6 = 72	12 × 7 = 84	12 × 8 = 96	12 × 9 = 108

0 × 10 = 0	0 × 11 = 0	0 × 12 = 0
1 × 10 = 10	1 × 11 = 11	1 × 12 = 12
2 × 10 = 20	2 × 11 = 22	2 × 12 = 24
3 = 10 = 30	3 × 11 = 33	3 × 12 = 36
4 × 10 = 40	4 × 11 = 44	4 × 12 = 48
5 × 10 = 50	5 × 11 = 55	5 × 12 = 60
6 × 10 = 60	6 × 11 = 66	6 × 12 = 72
7 × 10 = 70	7 × 11 = 77	7 × 12 = 84
8 × 10 = 80	8 × 11 = 88	8 × 12 = 96
9 × 10 = 90	9 × 11 = 99	9 × 12 = 108
10 × 10 = 100	10 × 11 = 110	10 × 12 = 120
11 × 10 = 110	11 × 11 = 121	11 × 12 = 132
12 × 10 = 120	12 × 11 = 132	12 × 12 = 144

Note for Teachers and Parents

Spell It Yourself is based on the belief that there is need for a new type of book which is neither a dictionary nor a conventional spelling book.

Most school children are encouraged to refer to dictionaries for words they wish to use in their written work. But school dictionaries have been compiled, in the first place, for the giving of definitions: the choice of words is usually dictated by children's problems of understanding rather than of spelling. As a result, many everyday words which nevertheless present spelling difficulties are not in school dictionaries, because children are sure to know their meaning.

Some of the commonest spelling errors are made in forming derivatives from root-words which in themselves are quite easy to spell. For example, a child probably knows—or could easily find from a dictionary—how to spell these infinitives: differ, prefer, happen, begin, come, singe, sail, dial, shop, gallop, argue, agree, queue, picnic, deny, tie, forget, fidget. But there will probably be nothing in the dictionary to help the child to the correct spelling of their present and past participles. How is he or she to know, for example, that the correct forms are 'shopping, shopped', and not 'shoping, shoped'? If the child remembers the doubling of that final consonant, how is he or she to know that the mistake of 'picnicing, picniced' must be corrected by writing 'picnicking, picnicked', and not 'picniccing, picnicced'? Other difficult and irregular word-derivatives not usually in dictionaries include plurals and the comparatives and superlatives of adjectives.

Certain spelling rules may be worked out, but most of these are confused by their many exceptions, and so are of limited usefulness, especially with younger children.

Clearly, children are likely to learn to spell correctly words which they are anxious to use in their own writing. In free writing, children are often not content to mis-spell, if they can avoid it; and they may waste much time, at the expense of the content of their written work, trying to discover the correct spelling of words they need. The usual school spelling-books of groups of words for memorization, children's own word-books, and most junior dictionaries cannot give proper guidance. The teacher often has little time to help with individual problems. It is hoped that this book, *Spell It Yourself*, will provide a useful tool, easy for children to handle for themselves as they need.

Spelling—with the exception of a limited number of the commonest words—seems a subject for individual learning: no two children wish to make use of exactly the same words in their written expression. This reference list, of nearly 8,000 root words, is based upon word-frequency in the upper classes of Junior and Middle Schools; but the list also includes many of the less common words which individual children may need.

In their written compositions children use words whose meanings they understand. They do not often need definitions of the words they cannot spell. Children's ability to read and recognize words is much greater than their ability to spell them; in this book they should be able quickly to find and identify the words they hesitate to spell. The order of the words is alphabetical, and if a child knows the first two letters—as he or she usually does—of the word required, the child can find in the Index the number of the page where he or she should look for it.

The alphabetical basis of the book provides useful training in the use of a dictionary. At the same time, *Spell It Yourself* makes a point of including many words which a school dictionary does not. Word-derivatives are usually shown by suffixes to the right of the columns which need only to be added to the root-words (see the Instructions).

In general, children learn best by finding out for themselves. In this book they will learn to look up words for themselves and to spell them correctly the first time, instead of making mistakes which have later to be corrected. They will steadily increase their written vocabulary, becoming more 'word-conscious' all the time. With this book at their elbow, and under the direction of a teacher aware of its purpose, they will be teaching themselves how to spell.

Index